ABOUT THE AUTHOR

Ronald Reagan and Nancy Reagan were America's president and first lady from 1981 to 1989.

Nancy Reagan was born in New York, raised in Chicago, and attended Smith College. During the summers before graduation, she worked in summer-stock theater productions. In New York, she appeared on Broadway, including in *Lute Song* with Mary Martin. She was signed by MGM and made eight motion pictures for the studio before leaving to marry Ronald Reagan. She is the author of a memoir, *My Turn*.

The SHERRY-NETHERLAND
FIFTH AVENUE AT 59TH STREET
NEW YORK 22, N.Y.

ELDORADO 5-2800

Wed. July 15

Dear Nancy Pants

Yesterday I went directly from the train to rehearsal — only stopping to check in here. Then suddenly it was two p.m. and rehearsal was over.

Back at the hotel I put in the call to you and then tried for Lou Wasserman — not in town! Sonny Werblin — away on vacation! Nancy Poo Pants Reagan — away out yonder! Eight million people in this pigeon crap encrusted metropolis and suddenly I realized I was alone with my thoughts and they smelled sulpherous.

Time was not a healer. — When dinner time finally arrived I walked down to "21" where I ate in lonely splendor. It was at this point with self pity coming up fast on the "rail" that you joined me.

Yes you and I had Roast Beef

2

ELDORADO 5-2800

The SHERRY-NETHERLAND
FIFTH AVENUE AT 59TH STREET
NEW YORK 22, N.Y.

although 21 is one of those places
we'll have to say "Well done". Medium
to them means "sponge off the blood".

Wanting only a half bottle of
wine we were somewhat restricted
in choice but we politely resisted
the "huxtering" of the wine steward
(who couldn't pick sweet milk from
vinegar) and settled for a '47 —
"Pichon Longueville". It was tasty wasn't
it? And I thought the most amusing
incident (and the nicest) was when the
lady to my left leaned over and
apologizing for her boldness introduced
the distinguished gentleman with her
(whose name of course we didn't hear)
It seems he is the publisher of
"Gourmet Magazine" and they were
so surprised (as they put it) to see
some one choosing a wine so carefully
And so intelligently in "21" of all places
that they just — had to remark about it.

ELDORADO 5-2800

The SHERRY-NETHERLAND
FIFTH AVENUE AT 59TH STREET
NEW YORK 22, N.Y.

I of course told them I wasn't really a gentleman I
just happened to marry a lady.
The people on our right we ignored
completely. A slick latin looking joker
with a doll "by Jelke out of jail" and
a Brooks Brothers character who was
evidently a 7 and 7 others junior partner
with plenty of loot he never could earn
for himself. I was sure the latin was
peddling the "broad" or a TV idea
until he raised his voice a little and
so help me he was promoting backing
for a "smart" old ladies home he wanted
to establish. He knew the world was
full of young couples burdened with
aging mommas who would leap at a
chance to stable them in his "nifty new
Home for Chronos", and the pay off would
top "South Pacific".

We walked back in the twilight
and I guess I hadn't ought to put us on
paper from there on. Let's just say I didn't
know my lines this morning.

Tonight I think we'll eat here at
the hotel and you've got to promise to let

ELDORADO 5-2800

The SHERRY-NETHERLAND
FIFTH AVENUE AT 59TH STREET
NEW YORK 22, N.Y.

me study — at least for a little while.

I suppose some people would find it unusual that you and I can so easily span three thousand miles but in truth it comes very naturally. Man cant live without a heart and you are my heart, by far the nicest thing about me and so very necessary. There would be no life without you nor would I want any.

I Love You

" The Eastern Half of US".

I Love You,
Ronnie

I LOVE YOU, RONNIE

The Letters of Ronald Reagan to Nancy Reagan

NANCY REAGAN

RANDOM HOUSE
TRADE PAPERBACKS
NEW YORK

RANDOM HOUSE TRADE PAPERBACKS and colophon are registered trademarks
of Random House, Inc.
This work was originally published in hardcover and in slightly different form
by Random House in 2000.

ISBN 0-375-76051-2

Random House website address: www.atrandom.com
Printed in the United States of America
2 4 6 8 9 7 5 3

For Ronnie

PREFACE TO THE
PAPERBACK EDITION

When Ronnie and I were married, on March 4, 1952, I had of course no idea what the future would hold for us. I only knew that I loved Ronald Reagan, and being his wife was then, as it is today, the most important thing in the world for me. "My life really began when I met Ronald Reagan," I said some years ago, and I also said, "I can't imagine life without Ronnie." Those statements, for which I was criticized back then, are just as true for me today as they were five decades ago—despite Alzheimer's, aging, and all the things that have happened to us. As the years have gone by and Alzheimer's has taken away Ronnie's ability to share our happy memories with me, his letters have come to mean even more. In fact, they are a kind of lifeline—preserving the past, Ronnie's wonderful voice and humor, his character, and his special way of seeing things and expressing himself. As they bring back Ronnie in his own words, they help me go on into the future. Many people have said to me after reading *I Love You, Ronnie,* "I had no idea Ronald Reagan was like that." But I of course always knew, and I treasure these letters especially because they bring back the Ronnie I have always loved.

As I write this preface to the paperback edition of *I Love You, Ronnie* on the eve of our fiftieth wedding anniversary, we are living out the love that began when Ronald Reagan walked in the door for our blind date in 1950.

In this book, I tell the story of a girl who wrote me a letter about thirty years ago, when Ronnie was governor of California. She was getting married and she asked my advice about how to have a happy marriage. I wrote back, saying I had no blueprint for marriage, how to make it happy and long-lasting, but that I thought "mainly you have to be willing to want to give." Now, as I reflect some more on the life Ronnie and I have shared, I would add that saying how much you love each other—to each other and also in letters that can be saved, read, and reread over the years—is a wonderful way to stay close. It is especially important in our busy lives to keep alive what really matters most: love, caring for each other, finding concrete ways to say it and show it, every day and in every way you can. It's what endures, after all, and what we retain and hold on to, especially in our hearts.

One of the things my life has taught me is how important it is to try to say "I love you" in ways that can be preserved, looked at, and read when you are alone or when there is adversity or when circumstances bring separation. In any case, as I think this book shows, saying "I love you" is one of the "secrets" of the happy marriage that Ronnie and I have shared. Ronnie's letters move me to this day. They are his gift to me across the years, and throughout the decades of love.

I am especially grateful that *I Love You, Ronnie* is coming out now in paperback, as I hope that more people—young people especially—will read it. It will be published on March 4, 2002, our fiftieth wedding anniversary, marking one of the days that I most looked forward to every year, since I always knew I would receive a special letter from Ronnie. He wrote me letters all the time, including on ordinary days and sometimes more than once a day, but our anniversary was always special. "Thank you for all my life and living and for happiness as complete as one can have on this earth," he wrote on March 4, 1967. "I more than love you. I'm not whole without you," he wrote on March 4, 1983. I treasure these and all the other letters from Ronnie. Having them and rereading them has helped me carry on in recent years, and I hope reading them will bring other people help and happiness as well.

—NANCY REAGAN

NOVEMBER 20, 2001

PROLOGUE

As I reread Ronnie's letters to me recently, getting ready to donate them to the Ronald Reagan Library, I realized in a new way how very special they are. I'd always intended them for the library, believing them to be of value to historians seeking to learn more about a former president. And yet as I read them once again, fishing around in the shopping bag I kept them in and pulling them out one after another, remembering and enjoying Ronnie's humor and style, his presence and his love, I was struck by how much they said about him—not just as a president, but as a man. And about us, the love we shared. The letters took me back in time, to the different moments of the life that Ronnie and I have shared for almost fifty years. And, once more, they brought Ronnie back to me, in his own words.

I realized how valuable the art and practice of writing letters are, and how important it is to remind people of what a treasure letters—handwritten letters—can be. In our throwaway era of quick phone calls, faxes, and E-mail, it's all too easy never to find the time to write letters. That's a great pity—for historians and the rest of us. If only people could see Ronnie's letters, I thought, they'd realize so much, including how wonderful it can be to take the time to write what you feel to those you love.

For all these reasons, I realized I wanted to do something more with Ronnie's letters than send them to the Reagan Library. I hated

the thought of their being stuck in a file there, read by a few schol-
ars and researchers yet not by the many people who love Ronnie
but don't have access to the Simi Valley archives. I decided I wanted
them to be able to read the letters before I donated them to the library. That way, all the people who admire Ronnie could share in
discovering the side of him that he's always kept hidden from public
view. That is to say, his private side. His heart.

Some of my royalties from the book will go to the Alzheimer's
Foundation, and the rest to the Ronald Reagan Presidential Foundation for the Ronald Reagan Library and Museum.

—Nancy Reagan
May 2000

ACKNOWLEDGMENTS

I am deeply grateful to Judith Warner for her help in the preparation of this book. And to Martin Garbus, my deepest thanks for his advice and friendship.

Many people at Random House handled this book with great care and sensitivity. J. K. Lambert deserves a special thank-you for his beautiful interior design. I am also especially grateful to Frankie Jones, Veronica Windholz, Benjamin Dreyer, Kathy Rosenbloom, Amy Edelman, Robbin Schiff, Andy Carpenter, Meaghan Rady, and Deborah Aiges.

And now, last but far from least, my editor and friend, Kate Medina. She was extraordinarily sensitive to what I was trying to do and very aware when I hit those periods when I just couldn't do anything and had to stop. However, when it was time, she would gently nudge me on, and somehow, with her help, I'd get it back together. I can never thank her enough for her patience and kindness.

March 4, 1981

Dear First Lady

As Pres. of the U.S. It is my honor & privilege to cite you for service above & beyond the call of duty in that you have made one man (me) the most happy man in the world for 29 years.

Beginning in 1951 Nancy Davis seeing the plight of a lonely man who didn't know how lonely he really was determined to rescue him from a completely empty life. Refusing to be rebuffed by a certain amount of stupidity on his part she ignored his somewhat slow response. With patience & tenderness she gradually brought the light of understanding to his darkened, obtuse mind and he discovered the joy of loving some one with all his heart.

Nancy Davis then went on to bring him happiness for the next 29 years as Nancy Davis Reagan for which she has received & will continue to receive his undying devotion forever & ever.

She has done this in spite of the fact that he still cant find the words to tell her how lost he would be without her. He sit's in the Oval office from which he can see (if he scrooches down) her window and feels warm all over just knowing she is there.

The above is the statement of the man who benefited from her act of heroism. The below is his signature.

Ronald Reagan - Pres. of the U.S.

P.S. He - I mean I, love & adore you.

Sunday

My Darling

Here it is — our day and if we were home we'd have a fire and "funnies" and we'd hate anyone who called or dropped in.

As it is I'm sitting here on the 6th floor beside a phoney fire place looking out at a grey wet sky and listening to a radio play music not intended for one person alone.

Never the less I wouldn't trade the way I feel for the lonliness of those days when one place was like another and it didn't matter how long I stayed away. With all the "missing you" there is still such a wonderful warmth in the lonliness like looking forward to a bright warm room. No matter how dark &

cold it is at the moment — you know
the room is there and waiting.

Of course when I say "you" anymore
I'm talking a package deal — you and
the two & a half year old you. Time goes
so slowly and I'm such a coward when
you are out of sight — so afraid something
will go wrong if I'm not there to take
care of you so be very careful

It's time to move on to the next
town now and every move is a step
toward home and you. I love you
so very much I don't even mind that
life made me wait so long to find you.
The waiting only made the finding sweeter.

When you get this we will be almost
halfway through the lonely stretch.

I love you

Ronnie

State of California
GOVERNOR'S OFFICE
SACRAMENTO 95814

RONALD REAGAN
GOVERNOR

Dear Mrs. Reagan

Your loving, faithful devotion has been observed these 19 (some say 20) years. There are no words to describe the happiness you have brought to the Gov. It is no secret that he is the most married man in the world and would be totally lost and desolate without you.

It seemed to me you should know this and be aware of how essential you are in this mans life. By his own admission he is completely in love with you and happier than even a Gov. deserves.

With Love & Appreciation
— Your In Law Gov.

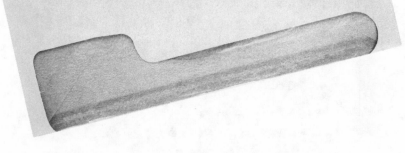

WESTERN UNION
TELEGRAM
W. P. MARSHALL, PRESIDENT

1958 MAY 18 PM 2 57
1201

The filing time shown in the date line on domestic telegrams is STANDARD TIME at point of origin. Time of receipt is STANDARD TIME at point of destination

LA128 OC148 LA393

(26)

L AYA140 PD=AQ ALBUQUERQUE NMEX 18 508PMM=

MRS RONALD REAGAN=

1669 SAN ONAFRE DR PACIFIC PALISADES CALIF=

=ONLY TILL TOMORROW MORNING BUT IF IT WERE ONLY A MINUTE
IT WOULD BE TOO LONG I LOVE YOU=

POPPA=

WESTERN UNION

FX-1201

W. P. MARSHALL, PRESIDENT

The filing time shown in the date line on telegrams and day letters is STANDARD TIME at point of origin. Time of receipt is STANDARD TIME at point of destination

.OA301 LG234

L.AYA554 PD=AQ ALBUQUERQUE NMEX 7 227PMM= 1955 MAR 7 PM 2 37

MRS RONALD REAGAN=

1258 NORTH AMALFI DR PACIFIC PALISADES SANTA MONICA CALIF CALIF=

DEAR NANCY GOING WRONG WAY BUT STILL IT IS ONE DAY

NEARER - I LOVE YOU=

RONNIE=

WESTERN UNION

TELEGRAM

[31]

W. P. MARSHALL, PRESIDENT

The filing time shown in the date line on domestic telegrams is STANDARD TIME at point of origin. Time of receipt is STANDARD TIME at point of destination

LA465 OC561

O SAA517 (L AYA691) PD=ALBUQUERQUE NMEX 22 557PMM=

MRS RONALD REAGAN=

1258 NORTH ARNALFI DR PACIFIC PALISADES CALIF=

WHAT DO YOU KNOW IT IS TUESDAY AND ALBUQUERQUE AND IM

IN LOVE WITH YOU=

CASH=

I Love You, Ronnie

On a boat, during the 1960s.

RONALD REAGAN

Dec. 25 - 1980

My Beloved First Lady

I'm supposed to be sitting here with my fingers crossed watching you open a package. I of course would be hoping it was something you really wanted; something that would show how much I love you. (Having the house painted won't do it)

But here I am — writing a letter again looking for words that will properly say it and those are hard to come by. Could you maybe give me a hint or two before next Christmas?

You see I have this problem. I miss you when you first leave the room. I worry about you when you go out the front door. Now this isn't good for me — not since my transplant. (You into my heart 29 years ago next March.) Without you there would be no sun, no moon, no stars. With you they are all out at the same time.

Bragging I'm not but believe me I do love you to the breadth & depth of all my being and I count all the ways I love you and they add up to greater happiness than I deserve.

Merry Christmas my Love.

Your Husband

Christmas 1980—it was perhaps the most important turning point in all of our lives.

We were due to leave for Washington in just a few days, and we both had a lot of things on our mind. They were different things, but still, they were there, and they preoccupied us. We'd been thrilled by the campaign and election night, and now we were planning for our new lives. Ronnie was thinking about all that it would mean to become president. He had always been very clear about his positions and where he wanted the country to go, but the idea of actually sitting in the Oval Office was daunting. I, on the other hand, was packing, getting ready to move us to Washington, clearing out closets and cleaning out the car port, which over the years I had filled with baskets and more baskets.

Christmas was Christmas nevertheless. We were there at home in California. Ronnie's thoughts were of those closest to him—our family, gathered around us for one last celebration in our house in Pacific Palisades. It was a strange time—the last time we would ever have Christmas together in the house where Ronnie and I had raised our children and built our lives.

On Christmas Day, our children and their families, plus Ronnie's brother, Moon, and his wife, Bess, came to dinner. We exchanged presents. Ronnie made a toast, as he always did, and he summed up, I think, what we all felt: "This toast is for all of us," he said. "Not for what we're about to become, but for what we've been, to each other, for so many years."

In the morning, I had found a wonderful letter, just as I almost always found a Christmas letter from Ronnie throughout the years of our marriage.

Christmas was, of course, a special occasion, but it wasn't the only time Ronnie wrote to me. From the earliest days of our marriage, and even before, Ronnie wrote to me all the time—beautiful letters, with descriptions of the world he saw around him; moving letters, filled with emotion, which deepened as we fell more and more in love.

No matter what else was going on in his life, no matter where he was, Ronnie wrote to stay in touch. I found his letters funny, warm, and imaginative. I loved reading them, and found myself looking forward to receiving them. Whenever Ronnie went away, I missed him terribly, and when his letters arrived, the whole world stopped so I could read them. I always loved not only what Ronnie said but the way he said it: the inventiveness and fun, the natural way he expressed his feelings and described the world around him. I saved every letter, every card, and every doodle.

Anyone who knows me well knows that I'm a saver. I always have been—and especially of anything having to do with my husband. Everyone teased me about it in the past, and grumbled about it when it came time to pack up all the things I'd saved and move. But then, when they were searching for things for the Ronald Reagan Library, they were suddenly very happy with me and the things I saved. For the librarians, the wedding clothes and baby shoes, the invitations and presents, and the boxes and boxes of photographs that I'd held on to over the years were nothing less than a treasure. But for me, the most precious thing of all has always been this collection of Ronnie's letters.

*On the pier Ronnie built at Rancho del Cielo,
near Santa Barbara.*

At first I kept them so that I could read them over again if I felt like it. Later, I kept them in a shopping bag. I brought them to Washington, where a lot more were added. It was a habit with Ronnie to write, to feel in touch, sometimes even when we were in the same room.

I have always loved them. In recent years, as Alzheimer's disease has gradually taken away Ronnie's ability to write, to remember, these letters have become even more important to me. They bring back so many memories.

The letters trace the story of our life. They begin as cheerful notes from the early years when we were dating. Then, in the first years of our marriage, they become deeper.

They were always a part of our life. In the fifties and sixties, when Ronnie traveled to make a movie or for General Electric, he sent me telegrams and long letters from across the country. Later on, he sent me funny notes from the California governor's office, then cards from *Air Force One*. Sometimes, when we lived in the White House, he wrote me letters from across the room.

I gave Ronnie cards—often, two or three or more at a time— for every holiday imaginable: Valentine's Day, Father's Day, Easter, even Halloween. But I wasn't good at putting my feelings into words. Writing came so naturally to Ronnie, but it didn't to me. He'd sit down, and, without drafts, without corrections, he'd come up with the most perfect and personal way of saying things— right off the top of his head. I was always struck by the way he did it, by the beauty of what he wrote and the ease with which he expressed himself. I wish I could have written back in just the same way.

—

Ronnie's letters tell the story of our courtship and how it matured from a Hollywood romance into a deeply loving and long-lasting marriage. It's interesting, I think, to see how our feelings grew over time, and to hear Ronnie express his wonder at his happiness. I believe he was able to share on paper feelings he wouldn't have been comfortable saying out loud, especially in those early days of our life together. His writing built an even closer bond between us.

Ronnie is not a complicated man. He's a private man—even, deep down, a shy man, I think—but not a complicated one. These letters are special because they give a lovely portrait of a man, in his own words. It is important, I think, to remember the happy times and the value of a life lovingly led, particularly now, given Ronnie's illness and the darkness that shadows every human being's existence. In the climate of today, I think it would be good for all of us to focus on the positive, the true, the things that really last, on character, humor, commitment, and love, and on the happy memories of a wonderful man and his life.

His letters were keepsakes in the past and have become my guardians of memory today. They recall happy times, and, above all, they preserve the voice of the Ronnie I love.

Santa Rita Hotel

NICK C. HALL
MANAGER

Tucson, Arizona

Mom.

Dear Nancy

Just a quick line from some where South of
Tucson (pronounced TOOSON) I'm balancing this on my
knee while I wait to ride gallantly over another
hill. I know now why the Confederates lost — they
were so d--n' hot in these uniforms they couldn't
fight.

Who said Actors are sissys — so far we have
injured three stunt men and I haven't seen them
do anything the rest of us aren't doing in every
shot.

Incidentally some characteristics of Mexican water
apply to Ariz. Of course it happened to me (story of my life)
Between the riding & the running I'm too busy to act.

Yesterday we ran about a weeks film and I
sort of think we have a good sl

There goes the "bugle"
me with ge

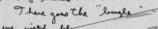

TUCSON
OCT 3
11 PM
1950
ARIZ.

GIVE—END
THROUGH
COMMUNITY C

UNITED
STATES
POSTAGE
3 CENTS 3

RETURN TO

SANTA RITA HOTEL
Tucson, Arizona

Miss Nancy Davis
941½ Hilgard
Westwood Village
L. A. Calif.

Ronnie's habit of writing to me began almost as soon as we started to see each other. In those early days, he was traveling all the time: on location for films (like *The Last Outpost,* which he shot in Tucson), to New York for TV jobs, around the country as president of the Screen Actors Guild.

Ronnie was on the road so much that we got to know each other slowly. And yet, when I opened the door to him for our first date, I knew that he was the man I wanted to marry.

We'd met in the fall of 1950 on a blind date—that is to say, a date that was blind for Ronnie but not for me. I'd seen him in pictures—and I liked what I saw. I was doing a picture—*East Side, West Side*—for Mervyn LeRoy, an old family friend, at Metro, when I saw my name on a list of Communist sympathizers. I went to Mervyn and said I was upset and asked if there was anything he could do. Later, it turned out that it was another Nancy Davis, but I was upset, so I said to Mervyn, "It's not right. You've got to do something."

Mervyn said not to worry; he would have the studio plant an item in Louella Parsons's column. The next day, I went to him again and said, "A little item in Louella Parsons isn't enough. My family's really upset." So Mervyn said, "I'll call Ronald Reagan. He's president of the Screen Actors Guild, and he'll be able to straighten things out. Come to think of it," he went on, "I think you two should know each other."

Now, that seemed like a very good idea.

"Yes, Mervyn," I said, remembering the handsome man I'd seen in movies, "I think so, too."

"I'll call him," he said. "And he'll call you."

But Ronnie didn't call, so the next day on the set, I said, "Mervyn, I'm *really* worried about this."

So Mervyn called Ronnie again.

Ronnie told me later that he couldn't understand why Mervyn was making such a fuss. But he called me that same day and asked me to go to dinner. "It'll have to be early, though," he said. "I have an early call."

I said, "Yes, I have an early call, too." I didn't—and he didn't—but we wanted to protect ourselves. He didn't even know what I looked like.

Ronnie was on crutches that night, having recently broken his leg in a charity baseball game.

"How come you moved in on me like this?" Ronnie would write me from a lonely hotel room years later, when he was away on one of his long trips for G.E. Why do people fall in love? It's almost impossible to say. If you're not a teenager or in your early twenties, you've gone on a lot of dates and met a lot of people. When the real thing comes along, you just know it. At least I did.

Looking back now, I still can't define what it was about Ronnie that made him seem so very perfect to me. I think we were just right for each other. And as the evening went on, I was more and more convinced. Ronnie had a great sense of humor, and he wasn't like any other actor I knew—or anybody else in the movie business. He didn't talk about himself. He didn't talk about his movies. He talked about lots of things, but not about "my next picture, my last picture . . ." He was a Civil War buff, loved horses, and knew a lot about wine. In fact, he had a broad knowledge of a lot of different things. I loved to listen to him talk. I loved his sense of humor. I saw it clearly that very first night: He was everything that I wanted.

That evening, we went to dinner at LaRue's, a glamorous "in" place on Sunset Strip where a lot of picture people used to go. After dinner, Ronnie told me that Sophie Tucker was performing at Ciro's. I said I had never seen Sophie Tucker. "Well," Ronnie said, "why don't we just go and see the first show?"

"Okay," I said. "Just the first show."

We stayed for the second show, and by then we had admitted that neither of us had an early call the next day. We saw each other the next night and went to dinner at a place out by the ocean, and I think we both knew afterward that we wanted to see each other again.

Things progressed slowly, though. We each continued to see other people for a while. Ronnie wanted to be sure, and, even though I'd never been married before, I wanted to be sure, too.

Whenever Ronnie traveled, I waited for letters and for other little signs that he was really interested. They came from time to time, and each one felt to me like a breakthrough.

There was, for example, the first time Ronnie asked me to come out to his little eight-acre ranch in Northridge. I don't think he'd ever asked anybody else there before, and I was thrilled. The ranch was out in the Valley, near a railroad track. It wasn't a fancy place, but it was very special to Ronnie. He'd built a ring there to ride in, and put in some hurdles to practice jumping, and that's what he did out there: rode and practiced jumping and bred horses with his partner, a very nice man named Nino Pepitone. It was a new world to me—you don't have many ranches in Chicago, where I was raised.

It was another breakthrough when Ronnie introduced me to his children, Michael and Maureen. I was so nervous about meeting them, so afraid that they wouldn't like me. Everything was a bit tentative at first. But as it turned out, we got along just fine. Soon, on every weekend and every holiday, when Ronnie went to visit the children, I'd go too. Maureen was often away at boarding school in those years, but Mike was around, and soon, every time we drove out to the ranch, he'd climb into my lap and stay there the whole time while I gave him a back rub.

Another breakthrough came when Ronnie introduced me to his mother, Nelle. She was living in a house that he'd bought for her and his father, Jack. Jack had died of a heart attack in 1941, and Nelle had been on her own ever since. She was an incredible woman. She visited men in jail and in the veterans' hospitals and talked to them, usually about religion. She screened films that Ronnie brought her for the tuberculosis patients in Olive View Hospital. Ronnie and she had always been very close, and now that she was getting older and living alone, he stopped by and had breakfast with her every morning.

He brought me along on one of these visits. Nelle and I got along well right away. She very clearly adored Ronnie and wanted him to be happy. Fortunately, she seemed to feel that I was making him happy—and that I could make him happy in the long term.

She very quickly sized up the situation between us. She said to me: "You're in love with him, aren't you?"

I said yes.

She said: "I thought so." And that was it. Nelle clearly saw where things were going, but she also knew that I would have to be patient.

The breakthroughs were, in fact, only baby steps. I just had to wait.

—

I was always so happy to get a letter from Ronnie in those early days. He wrote to me when he traveled—to stay connected, to reassure me, I think, and to let me know I was in his thoughts.

His humor, especially in difficult situations, comes through in his early letters, written before our feelings for each other had deepened and Ronnie began to write more directly about love. His letter from Tucson, Arizona, in 1950, for example, particularly shows Ronnie's humor about himself and the light touch he brought to describing the world around him. When he wrote it, we'd been seeing each other for about a year—long enough for me to be upset when he went away and for him to tease me for being "agin' it."

Television in 1950 was not what it is today. It was a new and not very highly considered medium. It was just beginning to attract some Hollywood talent, but it was considered a big step down from pictures. The work was live and low-budget and you rehearsed in basements.

Ronnie was sought out often for TV roles, but he turned most of them down. He didn't want to hurt his movie career by being type-cast as a TV actor. But he did sometimes go to New York to make guest-star appearances on shows that he liked.

He wrote me this letter on one of his New York trips. I can't remember what it was that he enclosed with it.

THE PLAZA
NEW YORK

[December 5, 1950]

Dear Nancy

Just enclosed this—thought you'd be interested. It was wrapped around some bread crusts the Guild office managed to smuggle into a TV mine where I'm being forced to work every day all day.

If this letter gets through tell all actors in the <u>free</u> world about this Siberia of thespians. Day after day in basement rehearsal halls we work and slave and in the few seconds of quiet between cues we can hear our ulcers growing. Mine is almost big enough to play a supporting part now but it is holding out for pictures.

They do have one custom that is cute though—<u>no prompter</u>. I have an extemporaneous address prepared for my first "memory loss"——it is entitled "Better Harry Cohen Yet" or "Pictures are Your Best Entertainment."

I have hatched an escape plot (used one of the eggs I've already laid) and expect to hit Calif. around the 17th or 18th if I can lose the "secret police" on a floating ice flow. I got this latter idea from a <u>new</u> TV show about some kid who outwitted a character named "Legree."

Gotta go——the guards are looking——through a viewer yet.

Ronnie

Our engagement photo; from MGM, February 1952.

When I met Ronnie, my picture career was really starting to take off. I'd come to Hollywood after a few years of working in the theater—first in small Smith College productions, then in summer stock during college vacations. My mother had been an actress, and the theater life had always appealed to me.

In those days, summer stock was very good training. You didn't act right away; first, you did a little bit of everything. That way, when you finally did get onstage, you had an idea of what went on offstage to get you there. I cleaned out dressing rooms (you could tell a lot about people from the way they left their dressing rooms); I upholstered furniture; I put on backstage music, I put up signs about the theater in the towns where we toured. My first part, when I did get onstage, consisted of the classic line "Dinner is served." It was all very, very good experience.

After college, I started acting on the "subway circuit" in the outer boroughs of New York. I even made it to Broadway once, working with Mary Martin and Yul Brynner in *Lute Song.* After someone with Metro-Goldwyn-Mayer saw me in the TV drama *Broken Dishes,* I was asked to come to Hollywood for a screen test and, as a result, was signed to a seven-year contract. At the time of my first date with Ronnie, I was filming *East Side, West Side* and working with Ava Gardner, Cyd Charisse, Barb Stanwyck, Van Heflin, and James Mason. For me, this was all very exciting. My role as a pregnant woman in *The Next Voice You Hear* came soon afterward, and I received top billing for the first time. It opened at Radio City Music Hall. The studio sent me to New York, and I took a picture of the marquee with my name on it. I was thrilled, to say the least.

In those days, if you were under contract to a studio, the studio was your life, six days a week. If you weren't making a movie—and I made eight for MGM—you were doing publicity for one you *had* made. That could mean traveling or even letting the cameras into your home, as I once did, when MGM set up some publicity shots of me moving into my apartment with a group of my studio friends. Pretty much all my friends were from the studio then. There wasn't much time to see anyone else.

When I was making a movie, I'd have to be on the lot at 7:30 A.M.—women always had early calls for hair and makeup—which meant that I had to be up extra early to drive myself to work. Unlike in today's world, you drove your own car to the studio. You knew that you had arrived when you could drive onto the lot and park the car there. Otherwise, you had to leave your car at the gas station nearby.

I'd stay on the lot until five or six every evening. And then, even on the days when I wasn't working, I'd come in and visit other sets.

That was one of the joys of being under contract: You could go onto any set and watch people work, which was something I liked to do, because you could learn a lot.

Ronnie was always supportive of my work, and he enjoyed my growing success along with me. When I was given my own dressing room—a sign that I had arrived at MGM—he gave me a gold key, with instructions to have it cut to fit the lock.

When I was given my own dressing room at MGM,
Ronnie gave me a key to it, along with this card.

Dear Nancy—

How about that dressing Room?—Well anyway if you'll take this to "Ruser Jewelers" they'll cut this to fit said dressing room.—Anyway it is To wish you a Merry Christmas

Ronnie

My career was bubbling along—and I enjoyed it. And who knows, I might have ended up with my name over the title for years, but then I would have ended up with no Ronnie. He was quickly becoming the center of my life. I had never felt so strongly about anyone before.

We dated all throughout 1951, and by the end of the year we were together all the time whenever Ronnie wasn't traveling. Whenever he was traveling, no matter how busy I was, I felt lonely and sad. We were just so happy together and so very comfortable in each other's company. We talked and laughed easily together, just as we had ever since our very first date. We very quickly saw that we both wanted to live the same way and liked to do the same things.

Like all other dating people in Hollywood in those days, we spent time at first going out to nightclubs like Ciro's and Macombo and LaRue's, but neither of us was really crazy about nightlife. The glamour was fun, but we preferred to be with good friends or to be at my apartment on Hilgard Avenue in Westwood, having dinner, watching television, and popping popcorn.

When we did go out to eat, our regular spot was Chasen's, which was very comfortable and less formal than Ciro's and Macombo. We always sat at the same booth there—that booth is now on display at the Reagan Library—and we always had a warm welcome from the restaurant's owner, Dave Chasen, and his wife, Maude.

Dave Chasen had been a vaudevillian. His first restaurant was a tiny little place where he made only chili, and it became a hit with the picture crowd. Eventually, though, a few of the actors who had backed him went to him and said, "Dave, you're giving us stomach problems. You can't just have us eating chili." They'd ask for chicken, and he'd run down the street and get some chicken someplace and bring it back. After a while, he just expanded.

I had a wonderful German woman named Frieda who came in to clean for me, and when she knew Ronnie was coming for dinner, she'd stay and cook dinner for us. He'd bring a bottle of wine.

Even after Ronnie and I were married and I'd stopped working, one thing never changed: I didn't cook. I still don't. For some reason, I was great with pancakes, waffles, French toast, but three times a day might be a little much.

Dave Chasen knew that I wasn't a cook, and I suppose it worried him a bit. So when Ronnie and I got married, he sort of took me under his wing. At that time, he was one of only two restaurateurs in town who went down to the meat-packing district and picked out his beef and supervised the cutting of it himself. "Nancy," he said to me, one day not long after our wedding. "Why don't you come with me and I'll show you how to pick out good meat and how to have it cut." Of course I said yes, and down we went. He was a dear man.

—

The quiet life that Ronnie and I had together wasn't like any he'd known before, but he liked it, and I did too. We started spending more and more time on the ranch in Northridge, sometimes staying out until evening to have dinner with Nino and his wife, Ruth. Nino would always call Ronnie when a mare delivered, and we'd rush out—it was so exciting and the foals were always so darling, so wobbly at first. Before long, Ronnie taught me to ride horses. ("Show him who's boss," he said to me the first time I got up on a horse. That's ridiculous, I thought. This animal knows perfectly well who's boss and it isn't me.) I took some spills—one, I remember, landed me right on my bottom—and I never became a great rider. But Ronnie rode, so I did too. I was, I suppose, a woman of the old school: If you wanted to make your life with a man, you took on whatever his interests were and they became your interests, too.

And so when Ronnie bought Yearling Row, his first ranch in Malibu, I went out and took it upon myself to paint his picket fences. That was no small job: It was a 360-acre ranch! I painted into the sunset, until there wasn't a single streak of light left in the sky. At the end of each day, I'd take off my blue jeans and they'd be so caked with paint that they'd almost stand up on their own. My skin would be in similar condition. One day my makeup man at Metro said to me: "I have to tell you, Nancy, this is a first: I've never had to make up an actress at Metro and first remove paint from her face."

The house at the ranch was really pretty sad; it had no foundation, and it listed, but we tried to clean it up so it was a little usable. It had what we called a pool—a pretty broken-down pool. But with all that land, it was a wonderful place to walk and ride. I remember, when Grace Kelly married Prince Rainier of Monaco, Ronnie read somewhere that the whole kingdom of Monaco was 360 acres, too. He said, "Do you realize that Yearling Row is the same size as Monaco, and you could be Queen Nancy and I could be King Ronnie?"

Ronnie loved to do outdoor work on the ranch. He was always looking around him and seeing new things he could do. He built all the fences, as he would again on the ranch we had later near Santa Barbara. There, when we'd go riding, he'd look around and comment on the trees, saying how he could make them look even better with some trimming. Then, of course, he would go up and trim the trees—and they *would* look better. We painted the interior of the Santa Barbara house and laid the tiles. He did the roofing. He just liked working with his hands—he always did.

After two years had gone by, marriage began to seem inevitable to both of us—and, I suspect, to Michael and Maureen as well. Gradually, I'd come to spend more and more time with them, and my relationship with them had become very easy and natural, which made me very happy. I'd go with Ronnie to visit them at Chadwick, their boarding school. I'd also be with Ronnie on Saturdays when he picked them up to go out to the ranch. In the car, we'd have lots of fun singing and playing games. Ronnie taught us all "La Marseillaise," and Mermie and I sang a duet to "You're Just in Love" until, I think, we drove Mike and Ronnie crazy. Ronnie had a game where he'd pretend he was a little dog and could listen in on conversations from the telephone wires, and he'd make up all these stories of conversations he'd supposedly heard. Ronnie had a station wagon, and we played another game where whoever saw another station wagon first had to yell it out. I don't know why we didn't have an accident—we were so busy looking for these station wagons. Then, on the drive home from the ranch, we'd always stop and get a bottle of apple cider at a place Ronnie had discovered, and ice cream cones—not to be consumed at the same time, of course!

It's difficult to get ready to marry a man who has children—difficult for both sides, because the children have their own feelings. But I think we all handled it well. I remember when Maureen named the first foal born at Yearling Row Nancy D. It thrilled me. I felt that it was a very warm welcome into the family.

By the end of 1951, wherever we went, reporters popped the question "When are you going to get married?" I was beginning to wonder, too, and I was beginning to get impatient. I knew that I wanted to spend my life with Ronnie, and time was marching on. I had long conversations about it with my mother, who listened and advised me. We were always very close, and I couldn't really talk about these things too much with my friends.

But still, there was no proposal. So, in January 1952, I decided to give things a push.

"I think maybe I'll call my agent and see about getting a play in New York," I told Ronnie. As I recall, he didn't say anything, but he looked surprised. Not long afterward, while we were having dinner in our usual booth at Chasen's, he said, "I think we ought to get married."

I was ecstatic. I could have jumped out of my seat and yelled, Whoopee! But I could hardly do it at Chasen's.

So I answered calmly, "I think so, too."

Getting our marriage license.

At a Guild board meeting, Ronnie whispered to Bill Holden, "How would you like to be my best man at Nancy's and my wedding?"

Bill shouted, "It's about time!"

We announced our engagement in February. Before, Ronnie had called my father to ask for his blessing. Ronnie got three picture offers immediately after our engagement was announced, and we had a terrible time fixing a wedding day. Every time we thought we'd found a date, his work would get in the way. Finally, the date was set: March 4, 1952.

The press had been after us for so long, so many questions had been asked about when we were going to get married and where we were going to get married, that now neither of us really wanted a big to-do. We particularly didn't want reporters following us around on our wedding day. So we decided on a simple ceremony at the Little Brown Church in the Valley, with only our best friends, Ardis and Bill Holden, attending. The Little Brown Church was small and out of the way and seemed like a good place to be married quietly. Ronnie had found it; he belonged to the Hollywood Christian Church, but that was huge and would have attracted a lot of attention.

I remember the morning of our wedding day so well. At my apartment in Westwood, I got dressed in the wedding suit that I'd chosen at I. Magnin's: a gray wool suit with a white collar, which I wore with a small flowered hat with a veil. Frieda was there with me, and just before Ronnie came to pick me up for the ceremony, we called my mother. "Oh, Mrs. Davis," Frieda said when she got on the phone. "You should see her—she's so happy!"

It was true. I was very, very happy, and everyone seemed to be happy for us.

Ronnie arrived soon afterward with my wedding bouquet, and we drove to the church together. I was in the clouds as we walked into the church. In fact, I was so far off in the stratosphere that I didn't even notice that Ardis Holden was sitting on one side of the church and Bill was on the other. They'd had a terrible fight—but for me, none of it registered. I was in a happy fog, and I also managed not to hear much of the wedding ceremony. I missed it altogether when the minister said what I most wanted to hear: "I now pronounce you man and wife." I only came to when Bill Holden leaned over and said, "Let me be the first to kiss the bride."

"No, Bill," I said. "He hasn't married us yet."

Bill laughed and said, "Nancy, he has. It's all done."

Isn't it funny—it's always been like that for me: At very emotional moments in my life, it's as if I'm in a daze. For instance, I have almost no recollection of Ronnie's first inauguration. Now, when I watch tapes of the event, I think: I wish I could live that all over again.

After the wedding ceremony, we went back to Ardis and Bill's house and immediately called my parents and Nelle. We also called Michael and Maureen at Chadwick. The Holdens had wanted to give a party for us, and we'd said no. But they did have a photographer there, thank goodness—if they hadn't insisted, we wouldn't have any wedding pictures today. I, of course, still didn't know that they'd had this terrible fight and were not speaking to each other. We had dinner, a cake, and a champagne toast by Bill, and then Ron-

Visiting Ronnie on the set; with his mother,
Nelle, and my parents, 1953.

nie and I went to Riverside and spent our wedding night at the Old
Mission Inn. I remember that Ronnie carried me over the threshold
and that there were red roses waiting for me in the room. We stayed
just one night at the hotel, and the next morning we left for
Phoenix, to spend our very short honeymoon at the Arizona Biltmore with my family. Before we left, we gave my red roses to an elderly woman, who was sick and staying in the room across the hall
from ours.

On the road to Phoenix there were animal stands, where you could go in and see snakes and other local wildlife, mostly snakes. Terribly romantic—and we had to stop at every one! I wasn't mad for that part of the trip. These places were tiny, and when you went inside, you had to walk down a narrow passageway with snakes on either side. They smelled just awful. But Ronnie wanted to see the snakes, and he thought I should become familiar with them, because we were going to have a ranch.

After just a few days in Phoenix, we started back for Los Angeles, where Ronnie had a picture commitment. On the way home, there were high winds and they split the top of Ronnie's convertible. So the honeymoon ended with me on my knees in the front seat of the car holding down the top. We had to stop every once in a while so I could warm my hands.

Later on, quite a bit later on, I learned a funny thing about our wedding day. After all our precautions about keeping our wedding date and location a secret, Tommy, one of the captains at Chasen's, said to us: "You know, I knew when and where you were going to be married." He'd overheard us talking at dinner, and he'd been there across the street from the church, watching. We never knew, and he never said a word to anyone. He'd just wanted to be near us. We found this kind of kindness toward us on the part of many people, over and over again in the different phases of our life together.

A month after we were married,
I visited Ronnie on the set.

When we first returned from Phoenix, we had two separate apartments—we hadn't yet had time to find a house to live in together. We lived at my place and Ronnie kept some of his clothes at his, and for a while he ran back and forth for suits and ties. Soon, however, we found our first home together—a single-level three-bedroom house in Pacific Palisades, which in those days was considered way out in the country. We paid $42,000 for it. Imagine what it's worth today! Every once in a while, I drive by to see it and the olive tree Ronnie planted in the front to be there when I came home from the hospital after having Patti.

I loved that house. It was the first house that I'd ever lived in. It had a library, a small study that we made for Ronnie out of one of the bedrooms, and a wonderful garden, where Patti liked to play in her sandbox. As she grew, she spent hours outside in that garden, sliding down her slide and playing in her sandbox. We had an English nanny, who loved to play the horses, and she and Ronnie had long conversations about the horse races. We went to the ranch often, saw friends, and had small dinner parties, but mostly we spent our time at home together on the weekends, doing things

From the scrapbook we made in the 1950s. Ronnie wrote
"our 1ˢᵗ home" under this snapshot of me in the library
of the house on Amalfi; November 1952.

around the house, watching TV, and eating popcorn, as we always had. A big neighborhood dog adopted us for a while, and I remember how she'd come over and watch TV with us too, sitting stretched out in a comfortable chair.

Our first years of marriage were not easy, though. Things were not going well for Ronnie in pictures. Hollywood had moved away from his style and image into a different feeling, which seemed to me darker and moodier. His career was really going downhill. He'd be sent scripts that were just awful, and he did a couple of pictures that were just awful.

We couldn't afford to furnish our living room. For special occasions, we'd reward ourselves by working on our house or garden—we'd paint a room, for instance. It was very, very hard for Ronnie. Yet it wasn't so different from what other young families getting started go through, and I had what I had always wanted: a husband I loved, and a family.

I had stopped working when Patti was born. Ronnie didn't ask me to—he would never have asked me to give up my career. It was

At home in the 1950s, in the house on Amalfi Drive.

For A Special Couple
Happy Anniversary

MOMMIE DARLING
It's a pleasure to congratulate
A special pair like ~~you~~ US
And wish ~~you~~ US happiness today
And in the future, too
Here's hoping that the dreams ~~you~~ WE share —
The memories ~~you~~ WE hold dear
Will mean still more to both of ~~you~~ US
With every passing year

& THEY WILL — BECAUSE
I LOVE YOU 2.3 X AS MUCH.

FROM ME — THE SCRIPT DOCTOR.

P.S. — I'M AT THE RANCH.
P.P.S. — I'LL SEE YOU TONITE.
P.P.P.S. — I'M LOOKING FORWARD TO IT
PP.P.P.S. — DON'T LEAVE WITHOUT ME.

Congratulations TO ME

And Life's Best Always — ~~BUT~~ FOR
I ALREADY HAVE THE BEST, THE MOST
BEAUTIFUL & THE SWEETEST WIFE
IN THE WHOLE WIDE WORLD.

Anniversary card.

my idea. I liked acting, but I had seen too many two-career Hollywood marriages fail. Ronnie was my whole life. I couldn't imagine life without him, and I didn't want to run the risk of anything happening to us. Also, I had seen my mother build a really happy marriage, putting a fine career as an actress aside.

When I left MGM, I had eight films behind me. I was proud of what I'd accomplished, and happy to stop there. I wanted to be a wife and mother. When we hit a dry spell financially, however, I felt I needed to go back to work, at least temporarily. I took a part in a

*Ronnie came to visit me on the set
of* Donovan's Brain.

film called *Donovan's Brain*, a science-fiction picture in which Lew Ayres plays a scientist who tries to keep a brain alive and is taken over by it. I see it often on TV now.

Ronnie made low-budget movies, accepted some TV parts, and even did a short stint as a Las Vegas nightclub host. His letters in this period were filled with wonderful descriptions of the places he was going and the people he was seeing. I found them so beautiful that I read them over and over again, even though they made me miss Ronnie so much.

This one—a real favorite—makes me weepy every time I read it.

THE SHERRY-NETHERLAND
NEW YORK, N.Y.

Wed. July 15 [1953]

Dear Nancy Pants

Yesterday I went directly from the train to rehearsal—only stopping to check in here. Then suddenly it was two p.m. and rehearsal was over.

Back at the hotel I put in the call to you and then tried for Lew Wasserman—not in town! Sonny Werblin—away on vacation! Nancy Poo Pants Reagan—away out yonder! Eight million people in this pigeon crap encrusted metropolis and suddenly I realized I was alone with my thoughts and they smelled sulphurous.

Time was not a healer.——When dinner time finally arrived I walked down to "21" where I ate in lonely splendor. It was at this point with self pity "coming up fast on the rail" that you joined me.

Yes you and I had Roast Beef although 21 is one of those places we'll have to say "Well done." Medium to them means "sponge off the blood."

Wanting only a half bottle of wine we were somewhat restricted in choice but we politely resisted the "huxtering" of the wine steward (who couldn't pick sweet milk from vinegar) and settled for a '47—"Pichon Longueville." It was tasty, wasn't it? And I thought the most amusing incident (and the nicest) was when the lady to my left leaned over and apologizing for her boldness introduced the distinguished gentleman with her (whose name of course we didn't hear) It seems he is the publisher of "Gourmet Magazine" and they were so surprised (as they put it) to see some one choosing a wine so carefully <u>and</u> so intelligently in "21" of all places that they just had to remark about it.

I of course told them I wasn't really a gentleman I just happened to marry a lady.

The people on our right we ignored completely. A slick latin looking joker with a doll "by Jelke out of Jail" and a Brooks Brothers character who was evidently a Fond Fathers junior partner with plenty of loot he never could earn for himself. I was sure the Latin was peddling the "broad" or a TV idea until he raised his voice a little and so help me he was promoting backing for a "smart" old ladies home he wanted to establish. He knew the world was full of young couples burdened with aging Mommas who would leap at a chance to stable them in his "nifty new Home for Chromos," and the pay off would top "South Pacific."

We walked back in the twilight and I guess I hadn't ought to put us on paper from there on. Let's just say I didn't know my lines this morning.

Tonight I think we'll eat here at the hotel and you've got to promise to let me study—at least for a little while.

I suppose some people would find it unusual that you and I can so easily span three thousand miles but in truth it comes very naturally. Man can't live without a heart and you are my heart, by far the nicest thing about me and so very necessary. There would be no life without you nor would I want any.

I Love You

"The Eastern Half of Us."

Though life was sometimes difficult in our early years together, Ronnie never let on that he was worried or upset. I knew he sometimes was—I just knew—but he never said anything outright. It just wasn't his way. Instead, he always tried to use humor to get through things.

In this letter, though we didn't know it yet, there was light at the end of the tunnel: the TV guest spot Ronnie mentions for General Electric.

RONALD REAGAN

HOLLYWOOD, CALIFORNIA

Dear "Career Girl"

I missed you!

There is nothing new to report on my own problems.

I missed you!

One offer at Las Vegas is for Feb., one for May. We are waiting to see the outcome of the "F.B.I." picture before accepting one or the other.

I missed you!

I may get a TV guest spot for General Electric soon.

I missed you!

Will see you as soon as this clam bake is over.

> *I love you—*
> *Pauvre Petite Papa*

P.S. It rained!

The Las Vegas nightclub job came to Ronnie in February 1954, through his agent, Taft Schreiber, at MCA. Ronnie was asked to spend a few weeks emceeing an act with a group of performers called the Continentals.

Las Vegas wasn't really our kind of place, but we needed the money. We showed up, I recall, with a suitcase full of books. When the hotel owner went up to our room and saw them, he said, "I've never known anybody to come to Las Vegas with *books* before." He probably thought we wouldn't last.

But the Continentals turned out to be a very nice group of men—they were all married, and all of them had children. Ronnie got along wonderfully with them. In fact, while rehearsing, they got along so well that the group asked Ronnie to play a bigger role in their act. He did—and the show was a great success. People lined up in the street to get in.

After Ronnie's tour in Las Vegas was up, the hotel asked him to come back for Christmas, but he said no. No matter how well things had gone, we didn't want to be in Las Vegas for Christmas. Then, the Continentals presented me with a cup, because I'd never missed a

Dear Mommie

We Dident Buy
You Any Street
OR WALL so we Had
to Get somethino
This is so you
wont Get too tired
WHILE You WATCH US

Learn To Ride

We Love You & HAPPY
BIRTHDAY —

PATTI Poo & Ronnie Too.

Agoura, California   Tel: Superior 8-5274

A note from Yearling Row, our ranch in the 1950s.

performance—I went to each of the two shows every night for a couple of weeks. I never got bored. After all, as I knew from my theater days, every audience is different, and that makes for a different performance each time.

Normally, after a show, Ronnie and I would go back up to our room and read until it was time for the next one. But on the last night we decided to go instead to the casino. As we walked in, the nice hotel manager made a beeline for us, and cut us off.

"What are you doing?" he asked.

We said we just thought we'd do some gambling.

"No, no," he said. "Don't. I've seen too many people lose everything here. Go back!"

"We're only going to gamble twenty dollars," Ronnie told him.

"Well, okay," the manager said. "But no more!"

He was really looking out for us. It felt like a nice way to leave Las Vegas, capping off happily what could have been a very difficult time.

RONALD REAGAN

M — IS FOR THE MISERY OF WHICH I HAVE NONE.

O — MEANS ONLY THAT WITHOUT YOU I WOULD DIE.

M — IS FOR HOW VERY MUCH (WHEN WE'RE APART)
I MISS YOU.

M — IS FOR THE MILLION WAYS I LOVE YOU.

Y — YIPPIE !!! I'M SO HAPPY.

TAKE THEM ALL TOGETHER THEY SPELL

NANCY
MY WIFE, MY LOVE, MY LIFE.

HAPPY MOTHERS DAY !!

From an ADMIRER (IF YOU'RE CURIOUS
MY NAME IS AT THE TOP OF THE PAGE.)
+
I'M ON THE NEXT PILLOW OVER.

A Mother's Day greeting.

After the Las Vegas trip, Taft Schreiber called with more good news: General Electric had come through with an offer for Ronnie to host a new television drama, *General Electric Theater*. Ronnie would introduce each episode, star in four programs a year, and act as "corporate ambassador" for G.E., going around the country visiting plants and offices. The idea was that he could talk about G.E. products and answer questions about the company to G.E. employees and local businessmen.

It seemed like a great opportunity. TV wasn't considered so terrible anymore by the mid-1950s, and *General Electric Theater* promised to be a prestigious show. The G.E. job also would turn out to be a turning point in Ronnie's life—but we didn't, of course, know that then. We also didn't realize how much traveling Ronnie would have to do.

—

Ronnie's first tour for G.E. was scheduled for August 1954. But first, in July, he went to Glacier National Park, to make the RKO

At the Stork Club. I'm wearing the TUESDAY'S CHILD pin
Ronnie gave me when Patti was born, on a Tuesday.

western *Cattle Queen of Montana* with Barbara Stanwyck, director
Allan Dwan, and producer Benedict Bogeaus.

Patti was not yet two years old. When she was born, on a Tuesday, Ronnie had given me a TUESDAY'S CHILD pin, accompanied by a
note that read: "So you won't have to be too far from our 'Tuesday's
child,' ever. And because I intend to be as close to both of you as
Eggs are to Easter." It was very hard for him to be away from us both
that summer. And we were miserable being separated from him,
too.

And so he wrote, to cheer us all up. Often, he wrote about nature, which he loved, and I think he actually perceived it differently—more intensely, perhaps—than many people do. I remember, for example, how at the Santa Barbara ranch we'd ride uphill and he'd admire the way the trees looked in silhouette against the sky.

—

From my own experience in pictures I knew that sometimes on a movie set a team works well together, and sometimes it doesn't. As Ronnie described it, *Cattle Queen* was not a happy situation.

July 13 [1954]

A.M.

My Darling

The first day of shooting and like all first days I can't tell you good bad or indifferent. Everything is hectic and upset what with the truck caravan arriving from L.A. in the dark last night. Most of the morning was spent getting the trucks unloaded and the equipment straightened out. Ben B. is on hand so things can really get buggered up. I think Alan D. is trying to get some of the story holes plugged and this morning changed one scene "à la" a suggestion from "guess who." However, our opposition is B.B. himself so I only whisper in an off-ear and let them fight it out. So far "Lady S." is no help—taking the attitude of "who cares in these kinds of pictures."

However there is one golden glow warming my soul in this first sunset—I'm twenty-four hours closer to you. Last night was an-

My mother welcoming Patti, Ronnie,
and me to Chicago for a visit.

other one of those nights—just too beautiful to stand. So tonight I'll probably be looking at the Moon which means I'll be looking at you—literally and figuratively because it lays far to the South of this mountain top and that's where you are. That takes care of the "literal" part—the "figurative" part requires no direction, I just see you in all the beauty there is because in you I've found all the beauty in my life.

Please be careful and don't get too good at covering your own shoulder at night—I'd miss doing it. Be careful in every other way too—nothing would have meaning without you.

Now if two "Muffins" I know will exchange a kiss for me—my good night will have been said.

I love you
Ronnie

The constraints of working on a low-budget picture wore on Ronnie as time went on. He wanted to be at home. He missed us and all the little things we shared in our happy life together—things like the "Bermuda Bell," as he writes in this next letter.

The Bermuda Bell was something we had on the floor of our car that you could ring with your foot. It was one of our family rituals that in the evenings, Patti and I would sit at the little table in her room, and when Ronnie came home, he'd come up our circular drive and ring the bell, and we'd wave to him together from the window.

The frustrations of being far from home and unhappy in his work

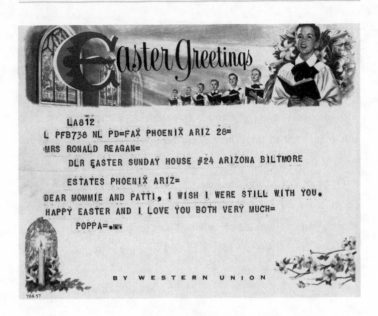

An Easter telegram from Ronnie to Patti and me.

were clearly weighing heavily upon Ronnie when he wrote the next letter. It was rare for him to sound so negative.

Sat. Jul. 17 [1954]

Dearest Nancy Poo

This has been the longest week in world history. Already I walk out the door and don't even bother to look at the scenery. The only scenery I want to see is a nursery window framing two faces when I jingle the "Bermuda Bell."

I don't know how the picture is going. We started in confusion and have managed to develop that characteristic to an unusual degree. B.B. is still defending his script, I'm still feeding suggestions to A.D. and those two then huddle and argue. Right now I'm waiting to go to work and the scheduled scene is one of those that needs changing the most. I'm quite interested to see what happens. In the meantime, what the h-l do I learn? B.S. just continues to go her merry way in the exclusive

RONALD REAGAN

company of two hairdressers and her maid. I wonder what picture she's making.

Having started in this somewhat downbeat vein—shall I continue? Well, the natives around here have a sort of "mid-1930's" approach to movie making. Everything has a price and we constitute fair game with a long open season. Let's start with the horses—at least that is what they are called. These scrawny goats were flushed out of the brush the day we arrived and if they ever had any training, they have short memories. The local cowhands claim they have produced their best—what they mean is, the best they'll let us use. Yesterday I did a scene mounted on my faded Palomino (which is the size of one of our Yearlings); the two locals playing extras with me were mounted on their own horses—both <u>registered thoroughbreds</u>.

When we do a scene the assistants yell "quiet" in a pleading tone entirely foreign to their usual manner. This is because the "locals" are restless and may quit and go home now that the novelty has worn off.

This, incidentally, is my first crack at picture making since the big switch to TV film work in Hollywood and it bears out everything we've ever said. First of all—getting a crew was a case of rounding up who you could find. The industry, as we have so often said, literally forced our technicians to seek work in TV and now we reap the harvest. Ben said there was a scramble to get enough guys for this crew—with no thought whatsoever of picking and choosing. Let's just put it this way—they and these horses have a lot in common.

Well now that is enough—any more of this inspirational literature and you'll envy me my stay in this pastoral paradise.

Your letter and Patti's enclosure arrived yesterday (Fri.) so you have some idea of the mail service. I'm lonesome and miss you both until it hurts. I still can't give you an exact date on homecoming. If I asked one of these boys for that information I wouldn't be able to coax them down out of the hills for hours—they wear a worn and harried look at this point. Let's just keep our fingers crossed and hope it is soon.

I love you so very much and miss you every minute. Be very careful of you.

Ronnie

Ronnie as host of General Electric Theater.

Ronnie hosted *General Electric Theater* from the fall of 1954 until the spring of 1962. During that time, our life together was lived in the happy moments stolen away from the long stretches when Ronnie was out on the road. He was away so much; I once figured out that if I added up all his time traveling, it came to almost two years—two years out of the eight he spent working for G.E.

I remember the shock the first time Ronnie went away on tour, because he was away for so long! Two months! At the beginning, I took Patti and went to see my family in Chicago. The time apart seemed to drag on and on. Ronnie and I were both so unhappy that after that tour, we never allowed ourselves to be separated for that long again. Ronnie told G.E. he simply could not go away for such an extended period, and he was able to arrange a new travel schedule so that he never had to leave home for more than two weeks at a time.

Even during the presidency, the longest we were ever apart was a week. That was when I went to London in July 1981 for the wedding of Prince Charles and Lady Diana. It was a hard separation, coming less than four months after Ronnie was shot. When the doctors told me they thought it was too early for him to travel, I'd originally said I wouldn't go to the wedding, either. But Ronnie insisted. He felt that after the shooting, I needed a change of scene. He was undoubtedly right—and the royal wedding was a treat. But I remember finding it very strange to be there on my own. In fact, I am never really happy, or entirely comfortable, unless Ronnie is nearby.

Ronnie has always been the same way, and so in the G.E. years, when he found himself in strange hotel rooms across America, he wrote to me of his loneliness.

ATLANTA BILTMORE
THE SOUTH'S SUPREME HOTEL

Sunday [March 20, 1955]

My Darling

Here it is—our day and if we were home we'd have a fire and "funnies" and we'd hate anyone who called or dropped in.

As it is I'm sitting here on the 6th floor beside a phoney fireplace looking out at a grey wet sky and listening to a radio play music not intended for one person alone.

Nevertheless I wouldn't trade the way I feel for the loneliness of those days when one place was like another and it didn't matter how long I stayed away. With all the "missing you" there is still such a wonderful warmth in the lonliness like looking forward to a bright warm room. No matter how dark & cold it is at the moment—you know the room is there and waiting.

Of course when I say "you" anymore I'm talking a package deal— you and the two & a half year old you. Time goes so slowly and I'm such a coward when you are out of sight—so afraid something will go wrong if I'm not there to take care of you, so be very careful.

It's time to move on to the next town now and every move is a step toward home and you. I love you so very much I don't even mind that life made me wait so long to find you. The waiting only made the finding sweeter.

When you get this we will be almost halfway through the lonely stretch.

I love you

Ronnie

Ronnie and I had a ritual, which began before we were married, for when he'd go away to film on location. On the day he was leaving, I would go by his apartment to pick him up and take him to the railroad station. As he finished his packing (he always, even in the White House, did his own packing; he liked to know just what he was bringing and where his things were), I would slip little notes and jelly beans in with the clothes in his suitcase. I'd drive him to the station, and I'd stay on the train until the very last minute. Then I'd get off and drive home feeling very lonely and very sad, and I'd knit him socks.

By the time we were married and Ronnie was traveling for G.E., I'd pretty well given up on knitting socks, but the rest of our routine was the same. Ronnie would leave California in the late afternoon, take the Super Chief train all the next day and night to

Chicago, then take the Twentieth Century to New York. He'd visit plants, make speeches, shake hands, tape episodes of *General Electric Theater,* and then begin the long train ride back. He was mostly unreachable while he was on the train, but when it stopped, as it always did, in Albuquerque, New Mexico, he'd be sure to hop off and run into the Western Union office in the station. Each time he passed through there, whether heading east or going west, he'd send me a telegram:

POWDER DOWN YOUR LIPSTICK. I AM ON THE DOWNHILL SIDE OF ALBUQUERQUE. I LOVE YOU.

DID YOU EVER GET THE FEELING YOU'D BEEN SOMEWHERE BEFORE? I AM GOING IN A CIRCLE. I AM ALSO IN LOVE . . .

PRESIDENTIAL TRAIN ON SCHEDULE. DON'T FIRE ANY SALUTES. I'M ABDICATING . . .

RONALD REAGAN

Feb. 14 - 1960

Darling Mommie Poo

Feb. 14 may be the date they observe and call Valentine's day but that is for people of only ordinary luck.

I happen to have a "Valentine Life" which started on March 4 1952 and will continue as long as I have you.

Therefore realizing the importance of this to me, will you be my Valentine from now on and for ever and ever? You see my choice is limited, a Valentine Life or no life because I love you very much.

Poppa

A Valentine's Day letter, from 1960.

"STOP AT RECOGNIZED HOTELS"

The Van Curler
Schenectady, N. Y.

THE GATEWAY TO THE WEST

Thurs, April 7

Dearest Nancy Pants

The enclosed clipping will give you an accurate picture of our arrival in Pittsfield last Sunday. Our hotel is the lighted building across the square.

I left N.Y. by train and arrived in Albany two hours late because of a wreck on the N.Y. Central the previous ni——— ———
we started our drive in ———
th— made———

The Van Curler
Schenectady 5, N. Y.

Airmail

Mrs. Ronald Reagan
1258 N. Amalfi Dr.
Pacific Palisades Calif.

——— but
——— thing interferes with these d—n "nut & bolt" fiestas.

DIRECTION, AMERICAN HOTELS CORPORATION

A letter Ronnie wrote from Schenectady.

MEET ME IN LOUISVILLE AND LET'S GET MARRIED . . .

STILL LOST BUT I THINK I'LL GET FOUND TOMORROW. DO YOU
SUPPOSE I LOVE YOU? P.S. I DO

And then, when he made it to Chicago, he'd see my parents and call me to check in. After that, we'd talk on the phone as often as we could. He'd write, and I'd wait, imagining him finding the little notes and jelly beans that I'd hidden among the clothes in his suitcase as a surprise. Doing things like that made me feel that I was still close to him when he traveled, and made Ronnie feel closer to me too. Nevertheless, as time passed, the separations became harder and harder to bear, and the long trips grew more grueling for Ronnie. Of course, no one ever heard the downside of things but me.

THE VAN CURLER
SCHENECTADY, N.Y.

Thurs. April 7

Dear Nancy Pants

The enclosed clipping will give you an accurate picture of our arrival in Pittsfield last Sunday. Our hotel is the lighted building across the square.

I left N.Y. by train and arrived in Albany two hours late because of a wreck on the N.Y. Central the previous night. Then we started our drive in one of the G.E. Cadillacs. We made it over the mountain weaving in and out of stalled cars and trucks scattered all over the road. Later that night three hundred and fifty cars and trucks were snowed in on that stretch of hi-way and hotels including ours were putting up cots to take care of the stranded week-enders.

Now you might think this would curtail some of our activities—but think not so. Nothing interferes with one of these d-n "nut & bolt" fiestas.

We arrived around 4:30 pm Sunday and by 7:30 were at a Country Club (Country Club??) for dinner with various and sundry G.E. executives (half the party were stalled around the country side & never made it) But _we_ made it and in the meantime had showered, changed clothes gone to _two_ radio stations for interviews and appeared on _one_ TV program. And this was a leisurely three hours compared to the schedule that began Mon. morning with a _press_ breakfast at 8 A.M. Try this with your shoes filled with snow.

It is, with some justification, I believe that I now employ my full register of eloquence to say—"I have had it!"

Tonite I address a banquet of "execs" (G.E.) here in Schenectady—and incidentally I resent it because this is my $\underline{3^{rd}}$ speech in this d-n town. I get in N.Y. tomorrow at noon and will film "openings & closings" all afternoon. But rest assured of one thing—only you have seen this bitter side. I have been a smiling picture of grace and warmth throughout each 18 hour day.

But all this is unimportant—what I really 'took pen in hand' to say was—I love you and miss you and I mean it differently than ever before. I've always loved you & missed you but never has it been such an actual ache. The clock is standing still and April 16th seems a year

away. I find myself hating these people for keeping us apart. Please be
real careful because you carry my life with you every second.

Maybe we should build at the farm so we could surround the place
with high barb wire and booby traps and shoot anyone who even sug-
gests <u>one</u> *of us go to the corner store without the other. I promise you—*
this will not happen again. How come you moved in on me like this?
I'm all hollow without you and the "hollow" hurts.

I love you
Ronnie

I felt hollow, too, whenever we were apart, but at least I was at
home. Life went on quietly in Ronnie's absence. I took care of Patti
and the house, and saw friends. When Patti started attending school,
I became very active in it. The John Thomas Dye School in Bel Air
was a lovely place, with fireplaces in all the classrooms and May Day
celebrations and hot cider and gingerbread at Christmastime. If
Ronnie wasn't traveling, he and I would cook hot dogs at the school
fair.

I was hoping to have another baby. But it wasn't easy. I had a mis-
carriage, and then when I finally became pregnant again, I had to
spend three months in bed, getting shots every week so that I
wouldn't lose him. The doctors told me that I'd be facing a cesarean
birth. Patti had been born by cesarean, too, so I knew what that
meant, and when our son, Ron, was finally born, on May 20, 1958,
I was ready.

Patti's birth had been another story altogether. Ronnie and I had been at the international horse show at the Pan-Pacific Auditorium when I'd gone into labor—without knowing it.

One of our horses was running, and I was so caught up with the show that I didn't realize I had started having labor pains. I just thought that Herman—I called the bulge Herman—was changing positions. I knew that the baby was breech, and we'd been waiting for it to shift, so I thought, Thank goodness it's finally happening.

"Herman is moving," I told Ronnie. He didn't really react. He just said, "Well, every time you feel that movement, squeeze my arm."

Then, at the end of the horse show, he said: "You're in labor."

"No," I said. "That's not possible."

"Yes," he said. "You've been squeezing my arm every fifteen minutes."

The poor man—I refused to believe it, so we drove all the way back to Pacific Palisades. We got undressed and got into bed. Only then did I decide he might be right. So we got dressed again and drove to the hospital.

My father never forgave me. A doctor's daughter not knowing she was in labor! He couldn't believe it. He thought I just should have *known*.

It was a long labor, and Ronnie was stuck in the fathers' lounge in a big leather couch with a spring sticking up through a hole. He sat there watching all the other fathers go up to the pay phone and say: "It's a girl!" "It's a boy!" And he just waited and waited. By the time he finally saw Patti, he was exhausted. Unfortunately, in those days fathers weren't present for births, and they couldn't even see their babies right away after they were born. And so when they finally brought Patti in to me, I was alone. I so would have liked to share the moment with Ronnie.

Maureen came to the house when I came home from the hospital, which made me very happy. She was eleven when Patti was born and had recently seen a film in school about cesarean childbirth. "Is *that* what they did to you?" I remember her saying.

———

Those were precious years, wonderful years of building a home and becoming a family. *General Electric Theater* brought us a new kind of security—and I think it's possible that the separations made Ronnie and me even closer. We cherished our time together all the more, knowing how lonely we felt when we were apart.

In the fall of 1955, we began construction on a new house in the hills of Pacific Palisades. General Electric decided to turn it into a showcase for the latest electrical appliances, and we found ourselves with more refrigerators, ovens, and fancy lights than we could use. The house consumed so much energy, and involved so much intricate wiring, that a special switch box had to be installed on the outside. Then, just before we moved in and right after the G.E. men had attached all the wires, some neighborhood kids came and pulled them all out. Holy Toledo!—as Ronnie used to say. All the wires had to be reconnected. In both our houses, Ronnie drew a heart with our initials in the cement of the patio—and at the San Onofre house it's there twice, on the patio and outside the bedroom.

Anyone who has ever built a house knows that nothing ever gets done just as, or when, it should, and this can drive you mad. But we were so grateful to have the financial security to *have* a new house,

*Another snapshot from the scrapbook. Ronnie wrote,
"The second house goes up." He loved being involved in the
construction of the house at 1669 San Onofre.*

and so glad to be together, that much of the frustration just rolled off us. And Ronnie, of course, did his part to make sure that we laughed our way through it all.

RONALD REAGAN
HOLLYWOOD, CALIFORNIA

Dear Mommie Poo Pants

The plumbers finish today—"honor bright hope to spit in the ocean"!

The slab gets poured next week—"hope to kick a dog"!

The carpenters start July 5—"I'll kiss your elbow!—your elbow??"

We should move in by Dec. 1—"That'll be the day!"

I left "Lucky" behind because she and our daughter were playing together and because it's too hot in Agoura for a fur coat you can't take off.

I love you and pledge my continued efforts at early morning machinery checks.

When I first opened the door?

Daddie Poo Pants

P.S. Never snuggled before—not even once.

Ronnie had started calling me Mommie when Patti was born. When I called her Patti Poo, he called me Mommie Poo. That led, somehow, to Mommie Poo Pants. Then to Daddie Poo Pants. The nicknames made us laugh—and becoming "Mommie" and "Daddie" also meant that our lives were changing, in very real ways. We were parents now—but we were also careful to never forget our marriage. We were always vigilant to not be "careless," as Ronnie put it in one letter, "with the treasure that is ours—namely what we are to each other."

Building a house brought Ronnie and me even closer together. It was a project we shared and both loved. Ronnie really liked all the details of building, the concrete steps involved. He took a very active role in planning the house. He built a model for it himself, which sat in the living room, and he went over every detail of the final design with our architect, Bill Stephenson. We decorated it together, carefully and slowly. I found some yellow couches for the living room that we both just loved, and they came everywhere with us afterward, including to the White House. By then, they were re-covered in a red print. At holiday times, instead of exchanging gifts, we finished rooms, built bookshelves and closets.

After a while, however, Ronnie got tired of giving these kinds of presents. For one birthday, he went to the jewelers instead:

RONALD REAGAN

Happy Birthday Mommie!

We've run out of rooms to buy. Anyway, how could we top the closet? I've gift-wrapped the living room, the bedroom, the dressing room, the den and the back bedroom. I'm tired of rooms for "presents."

Then you see I found out about these rocks—how would you like

Building the San Onofre house.

to get stoned on your birthday? ?——? I don't think I worded that right.

Anyway (again) please keep on having birthdays because I wouldn't know what to do without you. I think that's because I love you so much.

Happy Birthday.

Your surly Gunga Din

P.S. I truly do love you—mucher than that.

The first time we celebrated our anniversary in our new house was in 1956.

Nancy Poo Pants—

I should have married you so long ago this would be our Silver Anniversary. Anyway, I've had 25 years' happiness for each of the last 4.

I love you.

"That Man"

When Ronnie traveled now, I missed the little things most of all—the ways he loved and cared for me, how he would cover my shoulder with the blanket every night before we went to sleep, how we always slept on the same sides of the bed—him on the left, and me on the right—how we had breakfast on trays in bed together on weekends, which we started doing in our new house in the Palisades. I hated it even more then, when he went away. No matter how necessary it was for his work and the family, I never got used to it.

And sometimes, when we separated, I could get a little carried away. . . .

This led to a funny incident during the filming in 1957 of the picture *Hellcats of the Navy,* the only movie Ronnie and I ever made together.

Ronnie played Commander Casey Abbott. I was a navy nurse. He went down to San Diego to start shooting before I was called in. Then, when I showed up for my first day of work, I found this note waiting in our hotel room:

THE U.S. GRANT

Darling

Us old "Salts" always say "Welcome Aboard."—And My Goodness Are You Welcome!?!

We are working a while tonite so come on out to the war when you have "stowed your gear"(Heave Ho)

I love you
Commander Abbott

I loved working with Ronnie. Anytime I could be with him, I loved it. All went fine on the set—until, toward the end of the film, brave Commander Abbott had to take his leave and said good-bye to me. I began to cry—really cry. I guess there had been too many real-life good-byes in those days.

The director shouted "Cut!" and the scene had to be reshot.

The truth was, though, it was hard for both of us to say good-bye.

CARLETON LICHTY
GENERAL MANAGER

The U. S. Grant

HONORING A GREAT NAME

SAN DIEGO 12, CALIFORNIA

Darling

Us old "Salts" always say
"Welcome aboard". — And my goodness
are you Welcome !?!

We are working a while tonite
so come on out to the war when
you have "stowed your gear" (Heave Ho!)

I love you

Commander Abbott

A letter that was waiting for me in our hotel room
when I joined Ronnie to make Hellcats of
the Navy, *the only picture we made together.*

And as the G.E. years lengthened, it became particularly hard for Ronnie to spend long periods of time away from home and the family.

His telegrams now became more and more filled with longing.

WHAT AM I DOING HERE WHEN I WANT TO BE THERE. I MISS YOU & LOVE YOU.

WHY IS IT I DON'T GET AROUND TO SPEAKING MY MIND MORE OFTEN LIKE HOW MUCH I LOVE YOU AND HOW LOST I'D BE WITHOUT YOU.

HOW COME IT DOESN'T GET ANY EASIER. I MISS YOU VERY MUCH PROBABLY BECAUSE I LOVE YOU VERY MUCH.

As Ronnie traveled around the country for *General Electric Theater,* visiting plants and meeting with executives, he learned what was on people's minds. He heard people complain about the bigness of government and the burden of high taxes. The government, they said, was taking too much away from them. Ronnie knew what they meant. When we were first married, 90 percent of his salary had gone to the government. It got to the point where he had to turn down pictures because there was just no financial reason to make them.

Hearing other people's stories, hearing what bothered them and what they wanted, was a wonderful opportunity for Ronnie. He toured every single G.E. plant, walking miles and miles, talking and shaking hands with the plant workers. Afterward, he'd come home and tell me about meeting those people and how important it was to him.

*A family Christmas photo, from when
Ronnie was working for G.E.*

Soon, Ronnie's speeches became shorter and shorter, and his
Q & A sessions longer and longer. People didn't ask him about
toasters, and gradually, his talks became more political. He learned
a lot by listening to the hundreds of people he saw and hearing what
was on their minds and what was worrying them. He began to express his concern that excessive government regulation was drain-
ing the American economy and the free-enterprise spirit, which is
what he was hearing. His political views were changing. He'd gone
into the G.E. years a Roosevelt Democrat—and he'd remained a
Democrat even while petitioning Dwight Eisenhower to run for

president and campaigning for Richard Nixon. But with time, his political views had shifted more dramatically. And a new set of views formed that would eventually lead him to the governorship of California and then to the presidency.

Interestingly, General Electric never told Ronnie what to say or asked him to tone down the political content of his speeches until shortly before his show went off the air, under ratings pressure from the new color show, *Bonanza,* in the spring of 1962. And then, when G.E. told him to stop talking politics and start talking product, Ronnie simply refused. "I can't do it," he said. "When people ask me to speak, I can't switch lines completely and talk about appliances." He knew that when people went to see him, they wanted to hear what he thought—and to get the big picture.

With Mike, when he was living with us
in the San Onofre house.

Ronnie and Ron, summer 1962.

When the travel for G.E. came to an end, we had a few years, from 1962 to 1965, of relative calm. Ronnie taped a couple of television episodes—for *Wagon Train* and *Kraft Suspense Theatre*—then spent a season as host of *Death Valley Days*. He was at home in those years much more than he'd ever been before in our married life, and he was glad to have a full-time family life.

When he wrote this letter, in May 1963, he was in New York, working in television and collaborating with the coauthor of his early autobiography, *Where's the Rest of Me?* What was clearly in the forefront of his mind, however, was a troubling conversation we'd had the night before about the children.

Mike, who had come to live with us in 1959, when he was fourteen, was making some steps toward independence. Ronnie wanted to support and guide him but also felt that he, like all our children, needed the space to sometimes make his own mistakes. He was away so much that disciplining the children usually fell to me—as it often does to women whose husbands travel a lot. But the children always knew that he was there for them, and he always made his principles and beliefs very clear. In fact, years later, when Patti went to college at Northwestern and wanted to live in a coed dorm, it was Ronnie who surprised her by saying no. "I never expected to hear that from you," she said. "From Mom maybe, but not from you."

The Skipper was what we called Ron. He was such an easygoing child that we also called him Happy Jack.

RONALD REAGAN
PACIFIC PALISADES

Thurs. [May 24, 1963]

My Darling

Last night we had our double telephone call and all day (I didn't work) I've been re-writing the story of my life as done by Richard Hubler. Tomorrow I'll do my last day of location and then I'll call you and I'll tell you I love you and I'll mean it but somehow because of the inhibitions we all have I won't feel that I've expressed all that you really mean to me.

Whether Mike helps buy his first car or spends the money on sports coats isn't really important. We both want to get him started on a road that will lead to his being able to provide for himself. In x number of years we'll face the same problem with The Skipper and somehow we'll probably find right answers. (Patti is another kind of problem and we'll do all we can to make that one right, too.) But what is really impor-tant is that having fulfilled our responsibilities to our offspring we haven't been careless with the treasure that is ours—namely what we are to each other.

Do you know that when you sleep you curl your fists up under your chin and many mornings when it is barely dawn I lie facing you and looking at you until finally I have to touch you ever so lightly so you won't wake up—but touch you I must or I'll burst?

Just think: I've discovered I can be fond of Ann Blyth because she and her Dr. seem to have something of what we have. Of course it can't

Ronnie reading to the children,
at the San Onofre house, at Christmas.

really be as wonderful for them because she isn't you but still it helps to know there are others who might just possibly know a little about what it's like to love someone so much that it seems as if I have my hand stretched clear across the mountains and desert until it's holding your hand there in our room in front of the fireplace.

Probably this letter will reach you only a few hours before I arrive myself, but not really because right now as I try to say what is in my heart I think my thoughts must be reaching you without waiting for paper and ink and stamps and such. If I ache, it's because we are apart and yet that can't be because you are inside and a part of me, so we aren't really apart at all. Yet I ache but wouldn't be without the ache, because that would mean being without you and that I can't be because I love you.

Your Husband

Ronnie wasn't, of course, going to stay a private citizen for long. He had joined the Republican party in 1962. By the mid-1960s, he was an influential party voice, repeatedly asked by local leaders to campaign for their candidates.

In 1964, he was asked by Holmes Tuttle, a successful Ford dealer in Los Angeles, to make a fund-raising speech on behalf of Barry Goldwater at the Ambassador Hotel. That speech, which Ronnie wrote himself, went over so well that afterward, Holmes raised the money to have it televised and Ronnie's words attracted national attention. "You and I have a rendezvous with destiny," he said. "We can preserve for our children this, the last best hope of man on earth, or we can sentence them to take the first step into a thousand years of darkness. If we fail, at least we can let our children, and our children's children, say of us we justified our brief moment here. We did all that could be done." The televised speech brought in $8 million—more than had ever been raised for a candidate before.

Ronnie's running for office himself was the next logical step—or

Ronnie making a speech, with
Barry Goldwater in the background.

so some people thought. Holmes Tuttle put together a committee to support Ronnie for governor of California. At first, Ronnie said no. As in the past, when both Democrats and Republicans had asked him to run for office, he said he was a concerned citizen, not a politician. He was very happy with what he was doing. He'd just get into his own car and drive to wherever they wanted him to speak. He wanted to campaign for others, not promote himself.

But his supporters kept after him. Finally, Ronnie began to consider more seriously running for office, and we talked about it all the time. Ronnie agreed to run on one condition: that he could first go out and see if the people of California wanted him as their governor.

The response came very quickly. In San Francisco, the first city

March 4, 1963

My Darling

This is really just an "in between" day. It is a day on which I love you three hundred and sixty five days more than I did a year ago and three hundred and sixty five less than I will a year from now.

But I wonder how I lived at all for all the three hundred and sixty fives before I met you.

All my love
Your Husband

An anniversary letter.

we visited to test the waters, people were lined up around the block to meet Ronnie. We stood shaking hands for about four hours. The next morning when I woke up, I couldn't move my neck—shaking hands for so long had sent me into a spasm—and a woman had to come and wrap me in hot packs. But it didn't matter. We'd found the answer to our question, and now Ronnie's mind was pretty well made up. And of course, for me, whatever he wanted to do was fine.

Years later, people would sometimes say I pushed Ronnie into a career in politics. Nothing could be further from the truth, and saying that shows a real misunderstanding of Ronnie. For the fact is— and this is something that nobody, oddly enough, has ever picked up on—Ronnie has always been a very competitive person. He has never needed to be "pushed."

If you look back at his life, he very well could have stayed in Dixon, Illinois, but he didn't. He wanted to get out and become a sports announcer, which took some doing. Then, once he got out of Dixon, he kept on pushing. He got his position with WHO Radio in Des Moines in the middle of the Great Depression, and he was a very successful sports announcer. Later, when he was signed by Warner Bros. in Hollywood, he fought for the roles he wanted, and he fought hard for the parts that the studio didn't want to give him.

When the studio first turned him down for his dream role, playing George Gipp in *Knute Rockne—All American* (they said he didn't look enough like a football player), Ronnie drove home, dug out a few old pictures of himself in his college football uniform, and drove back to the producer's office. He won him over with the hard evidence.

He knew how to hold his own. When Errol Flynn, who was famous for stealing scenes, tried to push Ronnie out of a scene during the filming of *Santa Fe Trail* by having him placed behind a row of taller actors, Ronnie bided his time. Then, as the rehearsal progressed, he quietly scraped together a pile of loose earth with his feet, to create a little hill. When the cameras rolled, he stepped on top of that pile—and when it came time for him to deliver his line, there he was, clear as day, towering over the crowd, the tallest man in the scene.

Ronnie liked a challenge, and he wouldn't give up a good fight easily. It was never an ego trip. It was just a question of playing to win.

I supported Ronnie's decision to run for governor in 1966—not too much of a surprise. I always supported him in whatever he wanted to do. But as the campaign began, I felt a little uncertain about my own life in the political arena. It was a new and unfamiliar world for me. Early on, I warned the campaign people: "You know, I don't give speeches."

And they said, "You can take a bow, can't you?"

And I said yes, I thought I could manage that. Just that.

Ronnie's advisers knew what my soft spot was, though. Soon they came to me and said, "Your husband can't possibly get to all the small towns. It's too much for him; couldn't you help him out?" So I said yes, of course I'd like to help him out—I'd go to the small towns. But once I started, I was swept up in the whole experience. I found that I liked meeting the people, and it was exciting hearing what people said to me, seeing the character and

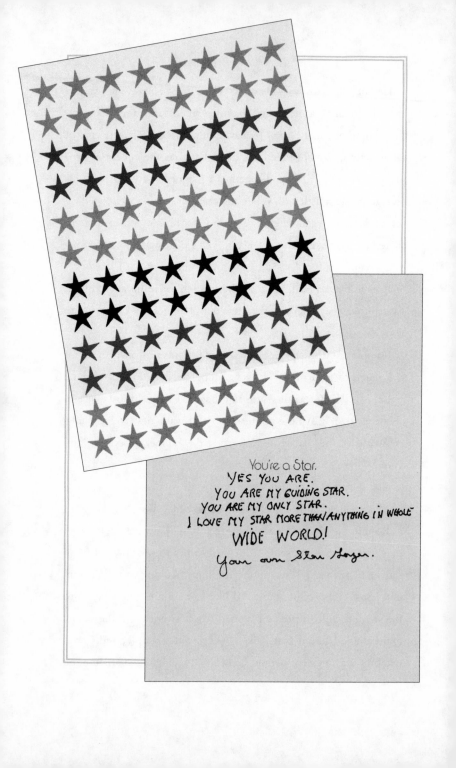

You're a Star.
YES YOU ARE.
YOU ARE MY GUIDING STAR.
YOU ARE MY ONLY STAR.
I LOVE MY STAR MORE THAN ANYTHING IN WHOLE
WIDE WORLD!
Your own Star Gazer.

friendliness in their faces, seeing all the new places. One place we went, I remember, was so small that there were no lights on the airfield. Trucks came out from the town and shined their lights on the runway. That shook me up a little. In *My Turn,* I mixed up the dates and said this happened during the 1976 presidential campaign, so I'm correcting it and a few other things in this book.

Ronnie had sworn off airplanes in the early years of our marriage, after two very frightening experiences. But once he decided to run for governor, he had to fly almost constantly for campaign appearances, and I worried about it all the time. Ronnie knew that I was worried, and it bothered him. He knew me so well—he understood that if anything had happened to him on a plane, I would have blamed myself for having gone along with the idea of his running for governor in the first place.

Ronnie wrote me the following letter in 1966. He felt he had to go out of his way to set my mind at ease about his having to fly, about the fact that his earthbound "groundhog days" (as he put it) of trekking by train and car were coming to an end. This thoughtfulness and sensitivity to me were typical of him, and of the way we were with each other. Also typical of Ronnie was the deep faith he expresses in this letter.

Ronnie has always been a very religious man. He was inspired in that by his mother. He has always believed, and has often said, that God has a plan for each of us and that while we might not understand His plan now, eventually we will. He often wrote to me of what was most important to him in spiritual terms, and I admired his faith, although I did not share the firmness of his convictions. I did, however, draw strength from his faith over the years.

PLANKINTON HOUSE
MILWAUKEE, WISCONSIN

Tues. Night

Dear Little Mommie

Knowing you (in addition to loving you) I think it's time to put something on the record. I've always known that someday my ground hog days would end, and now these political shenanigans have made

"someday" come around. <u>No one</u> talked me into this so <u>no one</u> should have any feeling of responsibility.

I have to write this because of all our talks about flying and because you'd try to take the blame personally if ever something did happen. That would be wrong. God has a plan and it isn't for us to understand, only to know that He has his reasons and because He is all merciful and all loving we can depend on it that there is purpose in whatever He does and it is for our own good. What you must understand without any question or doubt is that I believe this and trust him and you must, too.

What you must also believe is that I love you more and more each day and it grows more bright and shining all the time.

Good night, middlesize muffin, who is all the rest of me I need—

I love you

Poppa

GUESS WHAT NO PRIVATE DINING ROOM. THE VIEW WILL BE BETTER WHEN I FACE THE OTHER WAY. I MISS YOU & LOVE YOU—POPPA

ON WAY ONE MUCH IN LOVE HOT DOG SALESMAN DUE TO ARRIVE SUNDAY MORNING. LOVE POPPA

FINALLY SOLVED ARGUMENT OVER BEST WAY TO TRAVEL. DON'T. NO WAY TO AVOID MISSING YOU. I LOVE YOU

Ronnie being sworn in as governor, January 1, 1967. Something
was forgotten in the formal ceremony, so they had to
repeat part of it. Maureen and I are talking in the background,
and Ron is leaning on the desk, watching.

In November 1966, Ronnie was elected governor of California by a margin of nearly a million votes. We'd been out to dinner with friends on election night, and heard the results on a car radio on the way out to Ronnie's campaign headquarters. After all the anticipation and the hard work of campaigning, I felt a bit deflated for a moment. It sounds a little silly now, but I'd envisioned staying up all night listening to the returns and had been looking forward to it! But almost immediately afterward, I felt great joy at Ronnie's victory.

However, visiting our new "home" put a damper on my enthusiasm. The so-called mansion was located on a busy commercial street, right at a stoplight. Trucks would stop and shift gears and you'd hear their air brakes resonate throughout the house. The chandeliers would rock! There were times when you'd have to stop talking, because you couldn't hear over the noise. When my predecessor, Governor Pat Brown's wife, Berenice, took me on a tour of the house, she showed me a room in the back where she said she would go when the noise got so bad that she couldn't sleep. There was no place outside for eight-year-old Ron to play, and no way he or any of us could have fought our way out in case of a fire—all the windows were painted shut. The house had, in fact, been declared a fire hazard years earlier. And a hazard it was—full of dry rot, so that if a fire had ever started, it would just have taken off.

One Friday afternoon when Ron was home from school, the fire alarm went off. I grabbed his hand and we ran down the stairs and went outside. I said to the fire chief, "What happens if there's really a fire? How does my son get out of his room?"

And he said, "Oh well, Mrs. Reagan, it's very simple. He just goes over and takes a drawer from his chest of drawers and then runs over to the window and uses the drawer to push the window out." That did it!

That night, when Ronnie came home, I said, "We've got to move. I can't do my job as the governor's wife and fulfill my responsibilities to our children in this house."

So we moved. Sacramento didn't have many houses equipped to handle what's expected of a governor and his wife, but we did manage to find one, on Forty-fifth Street, that did just fine. The house itself wasn't big enough for any entertaining, but it had a wonderful backyard, with beautiful camellias and a pool, so we would wait until late spring or early summer and then we'd have our parties. We'd put a floor over the pool and have an orchestra and other entertainment, or in the hot weather we'd just have swim parties. People like Jack Benny and Red Skelton would come and perform, and I'd send notes around to all the neighbors, warning them about the noise and saying I hoped not to disturb them. Soon enough, the neighbors' kids would be crowding around, hanging over the fence to watch the entertainment. I'd invite them in, and they'd sit on the grass and listen with everyone else.

Ronnie, with instincts left over from his lifeguard days, was always aware of who was in the pool and what was going on. At one swim party, I recall, we were standing at one end of the pool when all of a sudden, without a word to anybody, he took off, dove in with his clothes and watch on, and pulled out a little girl. He stood in the water afterward, in his golf shirt and khakis, as she caught her breath by the side of the pool. Until that moment, no one else had even noticed she was in trouble.

I really loved that house. We paid rent for it—which we wouldn't have, of course, if we'd stayed in the governor's mansion—but it was

Ronnie jumped into the pool in Sacramento
with all his clothes on when he saw that
a little girl was having trouble.

well worth it. Unlike the mansion, the house on Forty-fifth Street was the kind of place where we could have a real family life. Ron built a tree house in the backyard and had friends over all the time. Often, they'd play football, and when Ronnie came home from work, he'd change his clothes and play with them. He told me, not long after we moved into the house, that the first time he came home and saw all the bicycles lined up out front, he knew that we'd made the right decision. And that, of course, made me very happy, because I felt I'd gone out on a limb in insisting we move out of the mansion.

We didn't have the ranch anymore—we'd had to sell it when we moved to Sacramento, because the taxes on it were more than Ronnie was going to earn as governor of California. But we did keep our house in Pacific Palisades. So, on the weekends and for holidays, we'd pack up Ron and our two dogs, Muffin and Lady, and go home. Patti was in boarding school and came home for holidays, too; and Mike and Maureen were grown up and living on their own. In the summers, we'd rent a beach house at Trancas, just north of Malibu, and they'd all join us there as often as they could. Having the whole family together made Ronnie very happy. I have lovely memories of those times.

Life was changing; each day was new. I found I really liked the job of being first lady of California. Ronnie and I gave dinners for returning Vietnam War prisoners, and I often visited wounded Vietnam veterans in local hospitals. I'd always end my visits by asking the men if they wanted me to call their mothers or wives. They usually said yes, and I'd go home with a list and start making calls, and the conversations would almost always be the same.

I'd say, "Hello, this is Nancy Reagan."

*With Patti and Ron on the
beach at Trancas.*

"Oh, come on now," the woman would say.

"Yes, it really *is* Nancy Reagan," I would say, and then I'd tell her that I had seen her husband or son in the hospital and that he sent his love. Then the woman would start to cry, and then I'd start to cry, and that's how we'd finish our conversation—in tears.

I also worked with the Foster Grandparents, a program I discovered at Pacific State Hospital, which I thought was wonderful. I still think it's one of the best programs I've ever seen, because it benefits both sides: children, who need love, and grandparents, elderly people, who need to feel wanted. They were matched up, and spent time together. I also wrote a Q & A column for a Sacramento newspaper, answering the questions that people wrote to me as first lady of California.

During this period—the sixties—I became more and more concerned about the problem of young people and drugs. I hadn't known anything about the growing drug problem in America until I started reading about it in the papers and began getting calls from friends. Some of their children had gotten involved with drugs, and some—like Art Linkletter's daughter and Charles Boyer's son—had died of drug overdoses. I felt it was a terrible tragedy for families and that it was growing in America. What kind of response would help? There was still such a stigma attached to speaking out about drugs at that time; people were embarrassed to admit that they or their families might have a drug problem. I wanted to see if there was something I could do about it as first lady of California. I thought perhaps I could use my position to break through the silence.

I'd never known this kind of public or civic life before, and I was learning so much! Many of the interests I eventually pursued when Ronnie became president started then—the seeds were planted, and I was getting some training in civic life, which I was very grateful for later on.

Ronnie and I now had new and different things to talk about every night at dinner. And yet, for us as a couple, the heart of our life had not changed, and in fact it never did; nor did our private time together. We'd come so far, lived through so much together: parenthood and home building, career reversals, life choices and changes. But in so many ways, we were the same. I still hated it when Ronnie left the room—and he didn't much like it when I did, either. We still shared everything. We spent as much time together as we possibly could. I just loved everything about this man!

Our fifteenth year of marriage coincided with Ronnie's first year in the governor's office, and the anniversary seemed to both of us like a particular milestone. I even wrote Ronnie a letter for it, which I found the other day in his desk drawer. Here are our letters to each other:

RONALD REAGAN

March 4 1967

My Darling First Lady

I'm looking at you as you lie here beside me on this fifteenth anniversary and wondering why everyone has only just discovered you are the First Lady. You've been the First—in fact the only—to me for fifteen years.

That sounds so strange—"fifteen years." It still seems like minutes, they've gone by so swiftly. If I have any regret it is only for the days we've been apart and I've had to awaken without watching you. Someday, you'll have to explain how you can be five years old when you sleep and for fifteen years yet. But then maybe it has something to do with my only being fifteen—because I wasn't living before I began watching you.

Thank you for all my life and living and for happiness as complete as one can have on this earth.

I love you so much and so much more each day.

Your Husband

My darling husband,

You beat me to it this morning 'cause I was going to write you—

I can never say what I really feel in my heart to you 'cause I get pud-dled up—and you always say everything so much better. But I too can't believe it's fifteen (16!) years. In another way tho' it seems like forever— I really can't even remember a life before you now. Everything began with you. My whole life—so you'd better be careful and take care of yourself because there'd be nothing and I'd be no one without you—

I love you so much—I never thought I could love you more than the day we were married but I do—and I'm so proud of you—every day—I could pop—It just keeps getting bigger and bigger—those poor other mommies—they don't have a you—but I do—and I hope you'll always have a me.

xxx

And when separations arose, we still took them very, very badly.

Dear Mommie,

The Gov. slept here—but not well. We have to stop this silly busi-ness. In fact I may buy a tent, load the jeep, take you away from all your friends & go live on our mountain. Then we'll only talk to each other.

I love you & I'll see you Sunday.

The Travelling, Non Sleeping Guv.

In Sacramento, Ronnie and I still looked after each other the way we always had. For me as a wife this meant, first and foremost, making a comfortable home for Ronnie and the family. For me as first lady, it also meant making the California governor's office a comfortable place to work.

It was far from that when Ronnie first moved into his office. In fact, the only thing Pat Brown had left behind was a tomahawk hanging on a wall. The carpeting was full of holes. Some of them had been patched—but not in the same color. It all looked awful!

I think that if you have pleasant surroundings, you can work better. I wanted to redecorate Ronnie's office and get it done for his birthday, on February 6, 1967. Somehow, with a lot of help, I did. Then I redid the conference room next door. Then I redid the outer office, where the secretaries worked. (Once you started fixing up one room, the others looked so terrible by comparison!) Then I fixed up the hallways. In storage, I found wonderful old pictures of Sacramento, and I lined the halls with them so schoolchildren could learn about the city when they came through to visit the governor's office.

I really enjoyed myself doing this, and Ronnie was just delighted. So was everyone else who worked in the office. They laughed when, as a finishing touch, I took a huge jar of jelly beans that a friend had sent to Ronnie and put it on his desk. But I also noticed that it was the first thing people went for when they came into the office to meet with him.

RONALD REAGAN

Dearest Mommie

When a fellow is in love he'll do the silliest things. — Like break-
ing promises and everything.

Anyway an Ermine cape seemed sort of impractical so please accept
this substitute.

There is no substitute for how much I love you and want you to have
the most wonderful Christmas "In the whole wide world."

I love you
Poppa

Everyone at San Onofre:
Patti, me, Ronnie, Mike, Maureen, and Ron.

Ronnie's tenure as governor came at a very difficult time in California. The campuses were aflame. Someone even tried to firebomb our house in Sacramento. We were in bed and heard a gunshot. Smart girl that I am, I immediately ran out on the balcony to see what was going on, making myself a perfect target. The police came running into our bedroom and said, "Put your robes on and come downstairs, and above all, *stay away from the windows!*" Downstairs, they found an unexploded firebomb made out of a champagne bottle. "Only in California," Ronnie said, referring to the fact that it was a champagne bottle.

I had seen Ronnie's sense of humor get him through a lot of difficult moments, but none more than when he met with enraged college students. They showed up to meet him disheveled, to say the least, and they were often very rude. Once, they greeted Ronnie outside a Board of Regents meeting by lining up on both sides of the sidewalk and giving him the silent treatment. Ronnie slowly walked the gauntlet in silence and then, when he reached the end, he turned around, smiled at them, put his finger up to his lips, and said, "Shhh!"

Another time, a student accused him of being out of touch. "You grew up in a different world," the student said. "Today we have television, jet planes, space travel, nuclear energy, computers . . ."

"You're right," Ronnie answered. "It's true that we didn't have those things when we were young. We *invented* them."

The student rebellion of the late 1960s and early 1970s was difficult for all parents, and we were no exception.

Ronnie never got truly angry—not at Patti or at Ron, Maureen, and Michael, or at me. It simply wasn't in his nature. At the White House, aides said the only way they knew he was really mad was when he took his glasses off and threw them on his desk. That's about as bad as things ever got.

At home, Ronnie and I disagreed so rarely that when we did it was a major event. As Ronnie says in the following letter, it kept him up half the night afterward.

RONALD REAGAN

Dear Mrs. Reagan

And you <u>are</u> Mrs. Reagan because <u>Mr.</u> Reagan loves you with all his heart. Every time Mr. Reagan sees the evening star or blows out the birthday candles or gets the big end of the wishbone he thinks the same wish—a prayer really—that so much happiness will go on and somehow be deserved by him.

It is true sometimes that Mr. Reagan loses his temper and slams a door but that's because he can't cry or stamp his foot—(he isn't really

the type.) But mad or glad Mr. Reagan is head over heels in love with
Mrs. Reagan and can't even imagine a world without her—

He loves her

Mr. Reagan

P.S. Mr. Reagan had to get up and take a sleeping pill halfway
through the night.

We tried never to go to bed angry. And we never let things smolder. We talked it out, and that was that.

RONALD REAGAN

PACIFIC PALISADES

Dear Wife,

*A few days ago you told me I was angry with you. I tried to explain
I was frustrated with myself. But later on I realized that my frustration
might have been a touch of self-pity because I'd been going around
feeling that you are frequently angry with me.*

*No more. We are so much "one" that you are as vital to me as my own
heart—with one exception; you could never be replaced with a transplant.*

*Whatever I treasure and enjoy—this home, our ranch, the sight of
the sea—all would be without meaning if I didn't have you. I live in
a permanent Christmas because God gave me you. As I write this, you
are hurrying by—back and forth doing those things only you can do*

and I get a feeling of warm happiness just watching you. That's why I can't pass you or let you pass me without reaching to touch you. (Except now or you would see what I'm doing.)

I'll write no more because I'm going to catch up with you wherever you are and hold you for a moment.

Merry Christmas Darling——I love you with all my heart.

Your Husband

Like any other couple, we didn't agree on everything, of course. But we never really argued. We worked on things. And I think that's why, beyond our love for each other, our marriage has always been so happy. What we felt was right out there, just as it is in the letters.

I tried to explain this once in a letter to a woman in Washington, D.C., who was about to get married and had written to me in Sacramento to ask if I had any tips for building a good marriage. "I'm very flattered that you wrote me, and I wish I thought I had a surefire formula for a successful marriage," I wrote back. Then I wrote,

I've been very lucky. However, I don't ever remember once sitting down and mapping out a blueprint. It just became "we" instead of "I" very naturally and easily. And you live as you never have before, despite problems, separations and conflicts. I suppose mainly you have to be willing to want to give.

It's not always 50–50. Sometimes one partner gives 90 percent but then sometimes the other one does, so it all evens out. It's not always

easy, it's something you have to work at, and I don't think many young people realize that today. But the rewards are so great. I can't remember what my life was like before, and I can't imagine not being married to Ronnie. When two people really love each other they help each other stay alive and grow. There's nothing more fulfilling than to become a complete person for the first time. I suppose it boils down to being willing to try to understand, to give of yourself, to be supportive and not to let the sun go down on an argument.

I hope that yours will be a happy road ahead. I'm afraid I've rambled a bit, and of course, I can only speak for myself. However, when I married, my life took on an added meaning and depth and truly began. I'm sure yours will too.

I knew it was very important for Ronnie, at the end of each day, to be able to put politics behind him and come home to his peaceful life with the children and me. He didn't like to go out after work, to stop off at Frank Fat's—the place everyone else in government went to for a drink. It had been the same way when he was in pictures—he never stayed around and had a drink with the fellows in the dressing room. He just came home. And in Sacramento, he wanted to close the door of his office and walk away. I think this helped keep him sane in the turbulent years of the sixties and early seventies, when the world seemed to go crazy. I think it also gave him a chance to think calmly, to sort out problems while he puttered around at home.

("Jess Plain Jess" in this letter is Jesse Unruh, a California state legislator and Ronnie's Democratic opponent in the 1970 gubernatorial election.)

EXECUTIVE MANSION
SACRAMENTO, CALIFORNIA

March 4 –70

My Darling

Sometimes it must seem as if the world is made up of Jess Plain Jess, Campus Slobs and Legislators—but that is only the outer layer.

Underneath is the place where I think about you round the clock and across the calendar—I spend most of my time there. I may get mixed up about March 2ⁿᵈ but never March 4—for 18 years it has been March 4 every day. Only this March 4 I'm 18 times as much in love as on that first one when I was really born.

I'm as grateful as I am in love.

Guv

Even though Ronnie's political career uprooted us to Sacramento, as it eventually would to Washington, our sense of having a solid home together never changed. We didn't feel the rootlessness that many politicians and their families say they experience. So long as we had each other, we *were* home. That feeling of home was something very special and necessary to Ronnie and is, I think, what he refers to when he calls himself "the most married man in the

Executive Mansion
Sacramento
California

March 4 - 70

My Darling

Sometime it must seem as if the world is made up of Jess Bavins jess, Campus slobs and Legislators — but that is only the outer layer.

Underneath is the place where I think about you round the clock and across the calendar — I spend most of my time there. I may get mixed up about March 2nd but never March 4 — for 18 years it has been March 4 every day. Only this March 4 I'm 18 times as much in love as on that first one when I was really born.

I'm as grateful as I am in love.

Ronnie

Ronnie's letter on our eighteenth wedding anniversary.

FOR MY SWEETHEART

I'll always call you Sweetheart
Because you'll always be
The dearest and the sweetest thing
In all the world to me.

I'll always love you, Sweetheart,
More than you could ever guess,
Because you are my everything...
My world, my happiness.

P.S. And it's all true - every single
word & then some.

From

A Valentine and a doodle.

world" in the next letter. Our home was his base, a source of comfort and strength. It was the same way for me.

He wrote me this letter to celebrate our nineteen years of marriage ("some say 20," Ronnie wrote, referring to the fact that in the year before our wedding, we were together so much that we might as well have been married).

STATE OF CALIFORNIA
GOVERNOR'S OFFICE

[March 4, 1971]

Dear Mrs. Reagan

Your loving, faithful devotion has been observed these 19 (some say 20) years. There are no words to describe the happiness you have brought to the Gov. It is no secret that he is the most married man in the world and would be totally lost and desolate without you.

It seemed to me you should know this and be aware of how essential you are in this man's life. By his own admission, he is completely in love with you and happier than even a Gov. deserves.

With Love & Appreciation
—Your In Luv Guv.

Being together made both of us feel whole, which had been true for Ronnie and me right from the start. It was why our lives had merged together so very naturally at first and why, after just a matter of months, it had seemed like we'd been together for years. It was also why, by the 1970s, when we were measuring our time together in decades rather than years, it was almost impossible to believe that we'd ever had separate lives.

(Birthdays became unbelievable for other reasons. "I don't care what the number is," Ronnie once wrote, diplomatically. "It only means more and more and more. I love you infinitely much.")

STATE OF CALIFORNIA
GOVERNOR'S OFFICE

[March 4, 1972]

My Darling Wife

This note is to warn you of a diabolical plot entered into by some of our so-called friends—(ha) calendar makers and even our own children. These and others would have you believe we've been married 20 years.

20 minutes maybe—but never 20 years. In the first place it is a known fact that a human cannot sustain the high level of happiness I feel for more than a few minutes—and my happiness keeps on increasing.

I will confess to one puzzlement but I'm sure it is just some trick perpetrated by our friends—(Ha Again!) I cant remember ever being without you and I know I was born more than 20 min's ago.

Oh well—that isn't important The important thing is I don't want to be without you for the next 20 years, or 40, or however many there are. I've gotten very used to being happy and I love you very much indeed.

Your Husband of 20 something or other.

State of California
GOVERNOR'S OFFICE
SACRAMENTO 95814

RONALD REAGAN
GOVERNOR

My Darling Wife

This note is to warn you of a diabolical plot entered into by some of our so called friends —(ha!) calendar makers and even our own children. These and others would have you believe we've been married 20 years.

20 minutes maybe — but never 20 years. In the first place it is a known fact that a human cannot sustain the high level of happiness I feel for more than a few minutes — and my happiness keeps on increasing.

I will confess to one puzzlement but I'm sure it is just some trick perpetrated by our friends —(Ha again!) I can't remember ever being without you and I know I was born more than 20 min's. ago.

Oh well — that isn't important. The important thing is I don't want to be without you for the next 20 years, or 40, or however many there are. I've gotten very used to being happy and I love you very much indeed.

Your Husband of 20 something
or other.

Twentieth-anniversary letter.

I've always said that my life began when I met Ronald Reagan. Ronnie often said the same thing about me. ("Thanks to you, I'm just eight years old today," he wrote on our eighth anniversary.) In the years preceding our marriage, he said, he'd felt lost. He hadn't been able to recognize himself as he made the nightclub circuit, dating starlets and enjoying being Hollywood's "most eligible" bachelor. He'd felt like he was wandering in the dark.

(He started calling me Senator, as he does in the next letter, after somebody kidded about my running for the Senate. It became a joke for everyone, and Ronnie jumped right on the bandwagon.)

RONALD REAGAN

My Darling Sen.

Two thirds of my life was spent in a holding pattern awaiting the happiest landing ever made: Now it is twenty-one years later— twenty-one years so wonderful I'd do it over and over again if each flight led to you. But I still wouldn't be able to tell you how much you mean to me.

I just want to start each day by opening my eyes and seeing you and end each day seeing you before I close them. In between times, I'll just look in my heart. You are always there.

There are no secrets in politics—it's a well-known fact that the Guv is very much that way about the Sen.

Very much in love—

The Guv

Ronnie always put special thought into his holiday messages. He could write mini-sonnets into the margins of greeting cards. And he never let a holiday go by without a card—or cards.

I'd find them waiting for me in the morning. I'd read and reread them. And, of course, I kept them all. A Thanksgiving card: "To the Woman of My Life—You Saved My Soul." A Christmas gift card: "If this were diamonds it still wouldn't pay the interest on the debt of love I owe you." A birthday greeting: "Life began for me when you were born . . . You are the light of my life and I never want you to go out." And a beautiful description of our marriage, one Mother's Day: "It is still like an adolescent's dream."

Valentine's Day always brought a particularly lovely letter.

Feb. 14 — 1960

Darling Mommie Poo

Feb. 14 may be the date they observe and call Valentine's day but that is for people of only ordinary luck.

I happen to have a "Valentine Life" which started on March 4 1952 and will continue as long as I have you.

Therefore realizing the importance of this to me, will you be my Valentine from now on and for ever and ever? You see my choice is limited, a Valentine Life or no life because I love you very much.

Poppa

As, of course, did our anniversary.

RONALD REAGAN

March 4, 1963

My Darling

This is really just an "in between" day. It is a day on which I love you three hundred and sixty five days more than I did a year ago and three hundred and sixty five less than I will a year from now.

But I wonder how I lived at all for all the three hundred and sixty fives before I met you.

All my love,
Your Husband

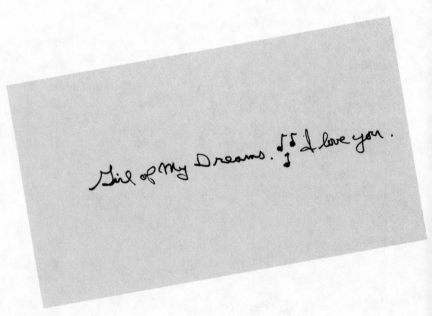

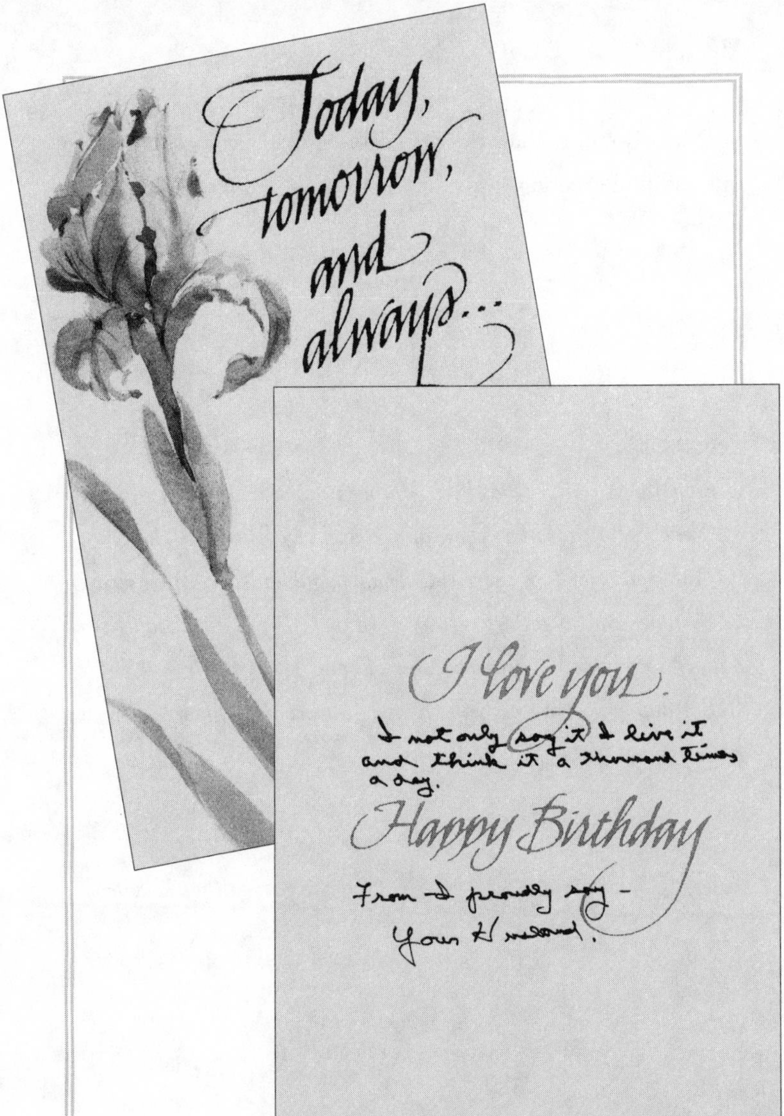

Today,
tomorrow,
and
always...

I love you.
I not only say it I live it
and think it a thousand times
a day.
Happy Birthday
From I proudly say –
Yours I beloved.

A birthday greeting.

When Ronnie's duties as governor limited his freedom to go out and find greeting cards, he improvised. He wrote, he joked, he doodled.

RONALD REAGAN

Dear Mommie

From Va. to Calif. it has been Mother's day, but it's hard to find a card at 39,000 ft. In fact there aren't even any flowers up there.

This then is my last resort—a common, old, ordinary letter written at ground level to tell you Happy Mothers Day.—It should be as happy as every day is for me because of you.

I'm happy you are my wife, happy you are a Mommie—I'm just plain happy.

> *I Love You*
> *Your Guv*
> *(You can just call me Excellency)*

RONALD REAGAN
PACIFIC PALISADES

Dear Mommie

No pretty card even—but then no card could possibly tell you how much I love you. In fact I can't find enough words myself to do that.

So multiply by a billion, double that and that's only the surface of

how deep it really is—"it" being my love (for) you. (I even start skip-
ping words when I think of it.)

I really love you mucher than that.

I.T.W.W.W. (In the Whole Wide World)
The Guv

Christmas was always a particularly special moment for Ronnie. But it was also a time for fun—and Ronnie had a lot of fun every year scheming, shopping, and trying to surprise me.

RONALD REAGAN

Dear Mommie

*The ring is because from the day of my birth my guardian angel in-
tended that someday I'd find you.*

*The gloves I hope will warm your hands as you have warmed my
heart for 25 yrs. + (that means plus). Of course on a really cold day I'll
<u>hold</u> your hands.*

*Box number 3? Well, for years Reno Nevada awarded each year a
pair of silver spurs to someone they thought the most of. You are hereby
awarded silver spurs for being the person I love more than anything in
the whole wide world. This award is permanent.*

*Merry Christmas and thank you for making every day a holiday
for me.*

"Guess Who"

P.S. I'll groom your horse for you too.

STATE OF CALIFORNIA
GOVERNOR'S OFFICE

Dear Poo Pants

It isn't very original. It doesn't show much imagination. But then if it was diamond-studded gold it wouldn't be as great a gift as the gift I got when I got you.

Merry Christmas with all my love.

Your Own Guv

RONALD REAGAN

Dec. 25

Dear Senator,

What to do for some one who just bought "everything"?

Well just get some more of "everything"!

I don't suppose Governors should write love letters to Senators, but in this case I'll make an exception.

Christmas has been a very special day for almost 2000 years. For the last 20 of those years it has been so special it has rubbed off on all the other days of the year. And that's because the Gov. has the Sen. I love you from the bottom of my heart—

The Guv.

"The Guv" hated the thought of buying me gifts that I wouldn't like. ("I hope you like it—don't worry if you don't—I can always take poison," he wrote one Christmas.) Rather than risk a big mistake, he would ask my friends if they had ever heard me express an interest in anything. Then my friends would call me for suggestions.

I always did my best to act surprised when I opened Ronnie's gifts—even though much of the time I wasn't surprised.

STATE OF CALIFORNIA
GOVERNOR'S OFFICE

Christmas 1971

My Dear First Lady

Here it is—Santa Claus time and no surprise for you. We've shopped early again (seems we do this more often lately).

Do you know I've never been really sure that you ever were surprised? There was always a thought that Amelia or Peg guarded your interests. But it didn't matter, you always seemed surprised and I'm not one to "look a gift getter in the surprise."

With nothing to put under the tree I thought of offering you all the stars for diamonds and the ocean breeze for perfume—but you already have those and besides I couldn't get them under the tree.

I could offer you my heart but I'd have to get it back from you first. There just isn't any thing to get for some one who already has everything I can afford.

If it truly is more blessed to give than to receive, then perhaps I should talk about what you've given me, because that makes you the most blessed person in these here parts.

Your gift to me is uninsurable. No appraiser can put a value on it.

A Valentine
FOR MY WIFE

A loving Valentine
For someone very dear,
Someone who grows still sweeter
With every passing year,
Someone who has given me
The best there is in life,
The one I love with all my heart --
My sweetheart and my wife.
It's true, It's true, It's true!
Your Own Guv

*How would he figure the market value of feeling a tingle of excitement
and anticipation every time I start for home? Or the way I can't help
but walk fast when I get there, hurrying for the first sight of you? Just
waking up becomes a warm glow because you are there—just as the
whole house is haunted when you aren't.*

*It's like fruit of the month or a lifetime subscription—a perpetual-
motion happiness machine. It starts off fresh and brand-new every day,
shining up my whole world.*

*Thank you for loving me and seeing that I'm smart enough to stay
very much in love with you.*

> *Merry Christmas,*
> *Your Husband.*

This Christmas letter seems particularly poignant. Our days in
Sacramento were coming to an end. Some of Ronnie's advisers had
started talking about his running for president in 1976, but I didn't
believe it. I thought we were leaving politics forever. It seemed like
the end of an era.

STATE OF CALIFORNIA

GOVERNOR'S OFFICE

Dec. 25–'74

Dear First Lady

*As you say—"we'd better use up this stationery." But "lame duck" or
"Ex" you are still my 1st Lady—now more than ever.*

These two little (and I do mean little) gifts do not necessarily go together as you will plainly see. One is for moving along and the other cozying down. Both however come with all the love I can put together.

You'll look cute and cuddly in one and gay and darling in "t'other".

I love you and because of that my Christmas is Merry—How about yours?

Poppa

Back home in the Palisades, Ronnie gave speeches and wrote a newspaper column, while I was busy with the children, their schools, and him. It was nice to be able to concentrate on our family life and each other once again. Ronnie was very happy. As he put it in this next letter, from Christmas 1975, that happiness felt to him like little less than a miracle. It felt that way to me, too.

RONALD REAGAN

Dec. 25–1975

Dear Mommie

The Star in the East was a miracle as was the Virgin Birth. I have no trouble believing in those miracles because a miracle happened to me and it's still happening.

Into my life came one tiny "dear" and "a light shone round about."

That light still shines and will as long as I have you. Please be careful when you cross the street. Don't climb on any ladders. Wear your rubbers when it rains. I love my light and don't want to be ever in the dark again.

I love you—Merry Christmas—

Your ranch hand.

On the deck at the San Onofre house.

We remained private citizens only briefly. Everyone but me, it seemed, simply took it for granted that Ronnie would run for president in 1976. He was willing—and I was certainly willing to support him, as always. And so before I knew it, we were back on the campaign trail, only this time Ronnie was expressing his views to a national audience. Ron traveled with us for a time, setting up microphones before campaign events as part of a school project. Maureen, especially, was delighted—she's a real political junkie. She played an active role in the campaign and was often by our side. Michael was there when he could be.

You might think that Ronnie's decision to run for president was a big turning point for our family or for us as a couple. While it was in certain ways, in others it wasn't. We didn't agonize over whether or not Ronnie should run. Quickly enough, it just became obvious that running for president was what Ronnie was going to do and that I was going to support him. If Ronnie was worried after he made his decision, he never let on. If I sometimes knew he was worried, it wasn't because he told me; it was just because I knew him so well. I never heard him express real fear or self-doubt; I don't think he really felt either. As I've said before, he liked a good competition. In any case, we didn't worry about the consequences once he'd made his decision. We weren't ones for family meetings—we just gradually came to a resolution.

In those days, running for president was completely different from what it's like today. There weren't the huge amounts of money you read about candidates spending now. We always had a lot of volunteers, lots of young people, and we really depended on them. We had a plane that we called the Yellow Banana, and we stayed in little nothing motels, real fleabag places sometimes. We spent little on food—Mike Deaver would often go out and get us Kentucky Fried Chicken for dinner. Once, I remember, in the South, we campaigned all day in the pouring rain. The rain ran up into our sleeves as we stood and waved. When we got back to our motel, soaked and frozen through, the manager refused to turn on the heat. So we finally had to leave, with all our staff and our baggage, and find another hotel room, with heat. That, for us, was a luxury.

The contact with the public was wonderful. However, we were losing every state. Everyone kept saying to Ronnie, "I think we're going to have to get out," but Ronnie just said, "No, I'm in it to the end." Then came North Carolina, and we won. And from then on Ronnie won every state.

The 1976 Republican convention in Kansas City was exciting. It was, in fact, the most exciting convention I've ever been involved with. For the nominating process, Jerry Ford's people put us way in the back of the hall, where no one could really see us. And yet when we went into our box on the last night, the people just wouldn't let

Ronnie sit down. They kept yelling, "Speech! Speech!" Ronnie tried at one point to speak, but they drowned him out; there was no way he could be heard. Frank Reynolds, the ABC newsman, came to the box to interview Ronnie, but it was impossible, and I heard him say, "This may not be the best journalistic derring-do, but I think I'll let him have this time."

The delegates' final vote was close, but we had known from the procedural vote the night before that President Ford would win the nomination. Now, after the final tally, Ford invited us onstage, and when we stood up front with the Fords, Nelson Rockefeller, and others, the response was amazing. The auditorium was packed. So many people were standing there, tears streaming down their faces, absolutely silent, waiting for Ronnie to speak. You could have heard a pin drop.

As we stood there, Ronnie whispered to me: "I don't know what to say."

I thought, Good Lord. I hope he thinks of something.

And then he gave the most wonderful speech. He talked about how he'd been asked to write a letter for a time capsule to be opened in Los Angeles for the tricentennial, a hundred years later. It was a call for unity and victory, and for the political will to strengthen our country, protect our freedoms, and save the world from the threat of nuclear destruction. The crowd shouted and clapped—it seemed they would never stop clapping.

The next morning, Ronnie met with a group of young volunteers. He quoted from one of his favorite poems, an old English ballad he had learned in school: "I will lay me down and bleed a while / Though I am wounded, I am not slain. / I shall rise and fight again." At a later meeting, which I also attended, he said:

The cause goes on. It's just one battle in a long war and it will go on as long as we all live. Nancy and I, we aren't going to go back and sit in a rocking chair on the front porch and say, That's all for us.

You just stay in there, and you stay there with the same beliefs and the same faith that make you do what you're doing here. The individuals on the stage may change. The cause is there, and the cause will prevail, because it is right.

Don't give up your ideals. Don't compromise. Don't turn to expediency. And don't, for heaven's sake, having seen the inner workings of the watch, don't get cynical.

No, don't get cynical. Don't get cynical, because look at yourselves and what you were willing to do, and recognize that there are millions and millions of Americans out there who want what you want, who want it to be that way, who want it to be a shining city on a hill.

I was crying, and a lot of other people in the room were, too.

I think there really was no doubt in anyone's mind that in 1980 Ronnie would win the nomination. It seemed preordained, really, after the 1976 campaign. He was ready, and everything seemed to fall into place. I remember his winning line in the debates: "There you go again," he'd say to Jimmy Carter every time President Carter started talking about the nation's "malaise." Everyone knew it was over after that. Ronnie had won the debate—and he would carry the election.

The country was ready for him. People were eager for someone to paint a positive, optimistic picture of the country. Ronnie made them believe that we had a bright future. He made people feel good about themselves and good about the country. And, quite simply, they liked him.

—

We traveled constantly during the campaigns, and often enough, we traveled apart. After our years of always being together, this was hard to get used to. As Ronnie wrote, in this lovely Valentine's letter just after the 1976 campaign, all we both ever really wanted was to be in the same room.

RONALD REAGAN

Feb. 14, 1977

Dear St. Valentine

I'm writing to you about a beautiful young lady who has been in this household for 25 years now—come March 4th.

I have a request to make of you but before doing so feel you should know more about her. For one thing she has 2 hearts—her own and mine. I'm not complaining. I gave her mine willingly and like it right where it is. Her name is Nancy but for some time now I've called her Mommie and don't believe I could change.

My request of you is—could you on this day whisper in her ear that someone loves her very much and more and more each day? Also tell her, this "someone" would run down like a dollar clock without her so she must always stay where she is.

Then tell her if she wants to know who that "someone" is to just turn her head to the left. I'll be across the room waiting to see if you told her. If you'll do this for me, I'll be very happy knowing that she knows I love her with all my heart.

Thank you,
"Someone"

If either of us ever left that room, we both felt lonely. People don't always believe this, but it's true. Filling the loneliness, completing each other—that's what it still meant to us to be husband and wife. Ronnie put it like this one Christmas:

RONALD REAGAN

To my wife——on Christmas day——'78.

Your mother raised a wonderful daughter——who became a most wonderful wife. It's amazing what that four letter word, "wife", covers when it's applied to you.

To my wife – on Christmas day – '78.

You mother raised a wonderful daughter – who became a most wonderful wife. It's amazing what that four letter word, "wife", covers when it's applied to you.

It means a companion without whom I'm never quite complete or happy. It means the most desirable woman in the world who gets more desirable every day. It means some one who can make me lonely just by leaving the room.

I live in a perpetual warm glow because of you. From the bottom of my heart I thank you for being my wife.

Merry Christmas and all
My Love
Your Husband.

P.S. The cavalry taught me "your leather" is supposed to match.
That explains the box.

Ronnie's 1978 Christmas letter and Christmas-tree doodle.

It means a companion without whom I'm never quite complete or happy. It means the most desirable woman in the world who gets more desirable every day. It means some one who can make me lonely just by leaving the room.

I live in a perpetual warm glow because of you. From the bottom of my heart I thank you for being my wife.

Merry Christmas and All My Love,

Your Husband.

P.S. The cavalry taught me "your leather" is supposed to match. That explains the box.

By the time of Ronnie's second presidential campaign, in 1980, we were a bit more used to traveling apart. We accepted it—there was a lot of terrain to cover. But that didn't mean we liked it.

(Thirty-three was Ronnie's lucky number. It had been his football number in college.)

Hey little Mommie—how come it keeps getting harder to say good-bye?

You'd think I'd be used to it but I'm not. I'm NOT REPEAT NOT going to get that way.

Maybe that job in Wash. wouldn't be so bad—you'd be right up-stairs.

I love you very much and miss you very much and I haven't even left home.

Don't talk to strangers—or open the door—just lock yourself in the closet and I'll let you out tomorrow afternoon.

I love you—(Special Agent) 33

That year, we even woke up apart on our anniversary.

RONALD REAGAN

March 4ᵗʰ [1980]

Good morning Honey. Isn't this an awful way to start an anniversary? I'm where I don't want to be and you're where (I hope) you wish I could be. And where I will be soon—the Lord and an airline willing.

A note and doodle from my "roommate."

Just think we were married 28 <u>minutes</u> ago. Yes, I know the calendar says years but what does it know? Time goes by faster when you are happy and I'm the happiest man in the world. I still think we should clone you. Then we'd leave the clone there and I'd bring you with me.

I've just figured out that if I keep on loving and needing you more at the same rate of increase for the <u>next</u> 28 years, every day will be valentine's day and I won't be able to let you out of my sight for more than 5 minutes at a time.

I guess when I was young I thought marriage might be this way for a while: I never knew it could go on and on, getting better and better year after year.

By now you must have figured out that I'm hinting, I love you more than anything in the whole, wide world. I'm running for re-election as your own totally dedicated husband.

> *I love you*
> *Your husband.*

P.S. I'm the fellow who sent the roses.

Campaigning consumes all your energy—mentally and physically. My memory of the 1980 campaign is just a big blur. I remember sinking into bed at night, absolutely exhausted. Ronnie would be so tired that he'd fall asleep right away. I usually would read for a while. Then I'd be hungry, and I wouldn't know what to eat. I didn't want to eat apples, because I was afraid that the crunching would wake Ronnie. So I'd eat bananas, which were soft and which, I figured, Ronnie couldn't hear. So then it got to be a joke between us. When we traveled, Ronnie would put bananas by my side of the bed.

I remember how I used to have fun with the press, too. On the campaign plane, I would take an orange and roll it down the aisle, and if it could get to the end of the aisle where the reporters were, I'd have won a great big victory. It got to be a routine, and then the press started putting up blocks—roadblocks—to stop my oranges. You can have a good time campaigning, and there can be camaraderie with the press—that is to say, as much as you want there to be.

—

On election night, in November 1980, we were at home in Pacific Palisades. I was in the bathtub, and Ronnie was in the shower. Ronnie loved to take long, long showers; he would think about his speeches and then write down his thoughts on 3 × 5 cards afterward. I had turned the TV up loud before I got in the tub so we could hear it better. Suddenly, I heard John Chancellor saying that Ronnie had won the election. I banged on the shower door, and Ronnie came out. We stood before the set wrapped in our towels and listened.

"I don't think this is the way it's supposed to happen," I said. It wasn't the way I'd envisioned it, at least. Next thing we knew the phone rang, and it was President Carter calling to concede and to congratulate Ronnie. We turned to each other in surprise. It was unusual for a president to call before the polls had closed. We couldn't quite believe it.

Yet, there it was—we were on our way to the White House.

The first inaugural ball, 1981.

Becoming president didn't change Ronnie at all. In the White House, he went on being the same man he'd always been—in Hollywood, in Sacramento, at home with me. Of course, his responsibilities were huge—and he felt them. But we kept up our private routines as much as we could. In Ronnie's rare moments alone, he still jotted off little notes to me, to say "Hello," "Where are you?" "I miss you," "I need you."

THE WHITE HOUSE

Dear Mommie, Poo Pants, 1st Lady, Nancy,

(How did I get so many wives?) Never mind. I love them each and every one. I know it's Feb. 4th—not Feb. 14th and not March 4th—but I can't stand it any longer. Happy Valentine's day!! Happy Anniversary!!

I love you,

Poppa, Poo Pants, 1st Guy, Ronnie

YOU ARE THE
REAL WHIPPED CREAM
ON THE PUMPKIN PIE
OF LIFE!

+ boy am I a dessert man?!

Praxy

I found this message on a Thanksgiving card on
my breakfast tray at the White House.

To Mrs. Reagan (That sounds beautiful to me),
  I'll be happy every minute I love you as my wife.
                    Your Husband—Your Happy Husband!

RONALD REAGAN

Welcome home little "Poopchin."
  I've missed you and can't wait to get home tonight.
  The song was sent to us by a lady who thought it was very appropriate for us. Of course she's right.
  The cups and saucers on your desk were another gift.
  I miss you, I love you, I miss you, I love you etc. etc. etc. Well, I'll be with you soon and if I haven't made it clear I really do love you.

                              Your Husband

On special occasions, I'd go over to his office and have lunch with him and we'd exchange our usual cards. I'd still get my beautiful Christmas letter and, though we always celebrated Christmas in Washington so that our Secret Service agents wouldn't have to leave their families, Ronnie still called my friends in California just before the holidays to find out what to buy me as a present. And no matter how busy he was with his duties as president, he always remembered our anniversary.

THE WHITE HOUSE
WASHINGTON

March 4, 1981

Dear First Lady

As Pres. of the U.S., it is my honor & privilege to cite you for service above & beyond the call of duty in that you have made one man (me) the most happy man in <u>the world</u> for 29 years.

Beginning in 1951, Nancy Davis, seeing the plight of a lonely man who didn't know how lonely he really was, determined to rescue him from a completely empty life. Refusing to be rebuffed by a certain amount of stupidity on his part she ignored his somewhat slow response. With patience & tenderness she gradually brought the light of understanding to his darkened, obtuse mind and he discovered the joy of loving someone with all his heart.

Nancy Davis then went on to bring him happiness for the next 29 years as Nancy Davis Reagan for which she has received & will continue to receive his undying devotion forever & ever.

She has done this in spite of the fact that he still can't find the words to tell her how lost he would be without her. He sits in the Oval office from which he can see (if he scrooches down) her window and feels warm all over just knowing she is there.

The above is the statement of the man who benefited from her act of heroism.

The below is his signature.

Ronald Reagan—Pres. of the U.S.

P.S. He—I mean I, love and adore you.

A Christmas greeting and a doodle.

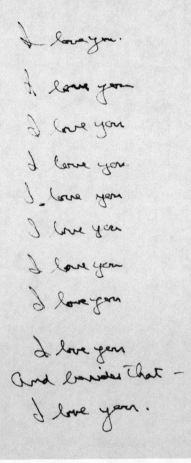

I had this note framed and keep it on my desk today.

While we were in the White House we spent as much time as we could together. Whenever we could, we made weekend trips to Camp David. Camp David! When I think about it now, it seems like another life—which, I guess, it was. It was such a wonderful place. I had heard so much about it and was so anxious to see it, and was happy to find it was all I had hoped for. Jimmy Carter had at one point considered selling it—he hadn't, thank God (he discovered that he liked it). But when we first started going out there, it needed some work. I did some gardening and some work on the cabins, which I really enjoyed. And Ronnie enjoyed himself in his own usual ways—being outside and riding, in particular. The Secret Service didn't want him going too far at first, but as time went by, he'd suggest adding a little more to the trail and then a bit more and a bit more, until, by the end, he had the kind of substantial ride he was used to.

Sometimes, just the two of us went to Camp David (that is to say, the two of us plus the Secret Service, the White House doctor, someone from the press office, and other White House staff—that's solitude during the presidency). Sometimes Ron and his new wife, Doria, would come, or a couple of close friends, like Charles and Mary Jane Wick and their children. But we never made a big social event out of it. What we really enjoyed doing there was relaxing, wearing blue jeans, reading, riding horses, watching movies—just generally doing the kinds of things that we'd always done on the ranch back home.

I think that's largely why we didn't find Washington strange or lonely the way many people who move there from other places say they do. We were still together all the time, and we were still us—with Ronnie on the left side of the bed and me on the right, waking up with our breakfast trays and our King Charles spaniel, Rex, a gift from Pat and Bill Buckley, jumping into bed between us. We added many new people to our lives who are still friends. Of course, living in the White House, if we wanted to make new friends, we had to reach out—just as anyone who moved to a new city has to do.

Making these new friends and bringing them home to Ronnie was part of the fun for me, and a big part of what I saw my job to be as first lady. There was also the work I'd begun in California: the Foster Grandparents and the drug program. The drug program, now on a national scale, took a lot of time. But it was also particularly rewarding.

Its best-remembered slogan, "Just Say No," had actually come into being during a visit to a school in Oakland. I was talking to a class of fifth graders when a little girl raised her hand and said, "Mrs. Reagan, what do you do when somebody offers you drugs?"

"Well," I had said, "just say no."

Somehow that caught on. I'm sure people thought it was a PR strategy that we'd worked out in the White House, but it really came about by accident. Obviously, it wasn't the whole answer to the drug problem, but it was useful and effective. It became a rallying point. You saw it on milk cartons and billboards, and you still hear it used today. I've always been proud of that, and of the work we did.

At the top of my list of duties as first lady, though, was taking care of Ronnie. I still considered that to be my most important job, as it had always been. For that matter, I do believe that taking care of the president is the most important thing a first lady can do—the essential thing, in fact, that she *must* do—because she is the person in the White House who knows him best. There are other people around who are supposed to take care of everything else—his scheduling, his briefings, his cabinet, his relations with the press. But the first lady is the only one who can really take care of the president's personal needs. She's the only one who really knows what's needed—at least, I think she should be.

Sometimes, though, at the most important moments in the president's life, you just can't be there. Try as you might, you can't always protect him from the outside world.

I'm getting off the horse at Camp David,
in the way Ronnie liked.

March 30, 1981, began like a perfectly normal day. Around noon, I went to a luncheon in an art gallery in Washington. When it came time for dessert, I suddenly had a strong feeling that I wanted to get back to the White House. I'd never felt anything like that before—and I haven't since—so I made my excuses and left. When I got back to the White House, I went up to the third floor, where we were in the midst of renovations. I was talking in the solarium with Rex Scouten, the chief usher, and Ted Graber, our decorator, when I saw George Opfer, the head of my Secret Service detail, standing at the bottom of a ramp that had been installed for President Roosevelt. He gestured to me to come down.

That's funny. I thought. Why doesn't he come up?

I went down.

"There's been a shooting," he said. "But the president's all right."

I was already headed for the elevator.

"He wasn't hit," he kept saying. "He's all right."

"George," I said, as we went downstairs. "I'm going to the hospital."

"You don't have to," he said. "He's all right."

"George," I said. "I'm going to the hospital, and you either get me a car or I'll walk."

It seemed to take forever to get to the hospital. Word of the shooting was out by that time, and the traffic had gotten very bad. When we finally made it there, Mike Deaver was waiting for me. "He's been hit," he told me. He suggested that we go into a little room and wait, which we did.

"Let me see him," I said.

"You can't see him now. They're working on him," he answered. "But he's all right."

The obvious question then was: "Well, if he's all right, why can't I see him?"

"You just can't," was the answer. "Not yet. They'll let you know when it's the right time."

"Mike," I said. "You've got to get me in. He's got to know I'm here. They don't know how it is with us."

Mike said he'd see what he could do.

I was terrified. I was also feeling like this couldn't be happening. John Simpson, a good friend, who was head of the Secret Service at the time, and Mike Deaver stayed with me. Outside the room, there seemed to be policemen everywhere, and they were yelling, "Get these people out of here!" There was so much noise. I kept wondering if this was what it had been like when President Kennedy was shot.

Finally, they came and told me that I could see Ronnie. I went into the emergency room and he was lying there with an oxygen mask over his face. When he saw me, he lifted it up and said, "Honey, I forgot to duck." He was the color of paper—just as white

At Camp David with Rex.

as a sheet, with dried blood around his mouth. I held back my tears and said, "Please don't try to talk. I love you." I wasn't allowed to stay for long, and I couldn't hold Ronnie's hand or get very close.

When it came time to take Ronnie to the operating room, I walked with him and held his hand while he lay on the gurney. Jim Brady was on a gurney just behind him. It was the first time I'd ever seen anybody who'd been shot in the head, and it was a terrible sight; his head was so swollen. I was taken upstairs to a larger room, where there were a lot of people and the television sets were on, and they asked me if I wanted to go to the chapel. I said yes. In the chapel, I saw Sarah Brady. It was the first time that I'd ever met her, you have to remember. We'd only been in the White House for three months, and I hadn't yet had a chance to meet everybody. She said to me, "They're strong men. They'll get through this." It was obvious that she hadn't seen Jim. And I certainly wasn't going to tell her.

I said, "Yes." We prayed together, and then I went upstairs.

As we waited, I looked out the window and saw how, in the buildings all around the hospital, people had thrown sheets out the window saying things like GET WELL, MR. PRESIDENT and WE LOVE YOU, MR. PRESIDENT. Every now and then, a nurse would come and report to me on Ronnie's progress. At first, the doctors were having trouble finding the bullet, which was a devastator bullet, the kind that explodes inside. One time, the nurse came and said, "We just can't seem to get it out. We may just have to leave it in." Well, that didn't sound so good to me. And then another time, she said, "They've found it, but the doctor is having a hard time removing it—it keeps slipping from his fingers." Finally, she came back and told me that the doctor had gotten it out; but I almost lost him then. The bullet had been lodged an inch from Ronnie's heart.

We were lucky—we didn't realize how lucky, in fact—because when Ronnie had arrived, all the doctors were in the hospital for a meeting. No one had to be called in. Everyone Ronnie needed was right on hand, and there was no waiting.

When Ronnie woke up, Ron and Doria were with me. Ron had been out touring with the Joffrey Ballet when he'd heard the news, and a plane was sent for them right away. The other children would arrive in the middle of the night, after the White House sent a military plane to pick them up.

When we walked into the recovery room, Ronnie had a tube down his throat. He felt like he couldn't breathe. He gestured to us, and wrote a note saying, "I can't breathe." I panicked and ran over to the doctors and nurses, saying, "He can't breathe!" But Ron just went over to him and calmly said, "Dad, it's okay. It's like when I went scuba diving. A machine takes over for you and does the breathing for you. It's okay."

But it was very frightening for all of us, including Ronnie.

I stayed at the hospital until the doctors said that Ronnie needed to sleep and that I should leave. I wanted to stay there all night, but the feeling was that it would be better for the country if I left and went back to sleep at the White House. Otherwise, people would have assumed the worst and there would have been panic. As it was, Ronnie's aides had to do all they could to calm the country down. The briefings made to the press were partial, to say the least. The assassination attempt was really a much closer call than people were led to believe at the time. Everyone was trying not to frighten the people in the country, but the fact was, Ronnie almost died. It was a miracle that he didn't. And I knew all along how serious things really were.

Looking back, I realize that when I went back to the White House, I was in shock. You never think your husband might be shot—you think that he might get sick, maybe, but not shot. And to me, even after it happened, it simply seemed unimaginable. That night, I slept on Ronnie's side of the bed. It made me feel closer to him somehow. And it kept me from reaching out and touching an empty space.

After Ronnie was shot, my desire to protect him just increased. His aides wanted to get him out there talking again as soon as he could. I kept saying he should be treated like any other patient and

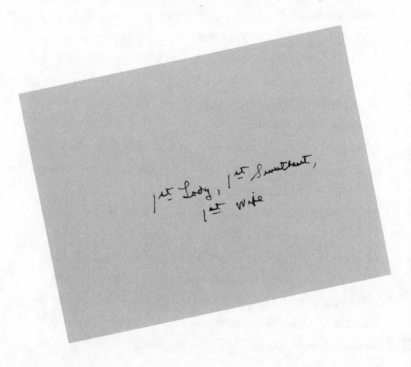

1st Lady, 1st Sweetheart,
1st wife

JUST a REMINDER THAT OUR WONDERFUL
BIRTHDAY SEASON WITH ITS HOLIDAY SPIRIT HAS
COME TO AN END — BUT YOU ARE STILL 29 TO
ME NO MATTER WHAT Isn't that
THIS SMART ALEC CARD SAYS,

carrying recession a little

too far?

Happy Day!

I Love you
Your Pres

A birthday greeting.

given time to recover. After all, we had almost lost him. He was a strong man and he was mending well, but he wasn't superhuman.

An incident like that makes you feel very fragile. The shooting only took two seconds. And you suddenly realize that two seconds is all it takes for your life to change entirely. Our security tightened after the assassination attempt, as it had to. Oddly enough, death threats increase after a shooting—it seems there's always somebody out there saying to himself, "Well, he didn't get him, but I will."

Needless to say, I was terrified. After the shooting, every time Ronnie walked out the door to make a public appearance, my heart would stop—and it wouldn't start again until he came back home safely. Ronnie knew how scared I was. But if he was frightened too, he never let me know it. As always, he was cheerful and optimistic. God had spared him, he believed; there had to be a reason why. By making jokes—as in this letter—he tried to take the edge off my fear.

THE WHITE HOUSE
WASHINGTON

Dear First Mommie

I'm in Wyoming, Montana,—or Nevada depending on what time you read this.

But I'll be at Camp David at 9:15 P.M Fri. Night. I'll be so glad to see you. I miss you—even when I'm asleep. This is a very lonesome place when you are someplace else.

Now I don't want this to come as a shock to you—but—well—

THE WHITE HOUSE

WASHINGTON

Dear First Mommie

I'm in Wyoming, Montana, — or Nevada
depending on what time you read this.

But I'll be at Camp David at 9:15 P.M.
Fri. Night. I'll be glad to see you. I miss
you — even when I'm asleep. This is a
very lonesome place when you are some place
else.

Now I don't want this to come as
a shock to you — but — well — well —
I'll just come right out with it — — —
I'm in love with you. There I've said
it & I'm glad.

You be careful. Don't talk to any
strangers & try to think kindly of me
because I love you mucher than
anything.

1st Poppa

A note before we were to meet each other at Camp David.

well—I'll just come right out with it—I'm in love with you. There I've said it & I'm glad.

You be careful. Dont talk to any strangers & try to think kindly of me because I love you mucher than anything.

1ˢᵗ Poppa

The assassination attempt made us realize how very precious our lives were. It made us all the more devoted to each other. I think this comes through very strongly in Ronnie's Christmas letter of 1981, written nine months after the shooting.

THE WHITE HOUSE
WASHINGTON

Dec. 25 1981

Dear Mrs. R.

I still don't feel right about your opening an envelope instead of a gift package.

There are several much beloved women in my life and on Christmas I should be giving them gold, precious stones, perfume, furs and lace. I know that even the best of these would still fall far short of expressing how much these several women mean to me and how empty my life would be without them.

There is of course my "First Lady." She brings so much grace and charm to whatever she does that even stuffy, formal functions sparkle and turn into fun times. Everything is done with class. All I have to do is wash up and show up.

There is another woman in my life who does things I don't always get to see but I hear about them and sometimes see photos of her doing them. She takes an abandoned child in her arms on a hospital visit. The look on her face only the Madonna could match. The look on the child's face is one of adoration. I know because I adore her too.

She bends over a wheelchair or bed to touch an elderly invalid with tenderness and compassion just as she fills my life with warmth and love.

There is another gal I love who is a nest builder. If she were stuck three days in a hotel room she'd manage to make it home sweet home. She moves things around—looks at it—straightens this and that and you wonder why it wasn't that way in the first place.

I'm also crazy about the girl who goes to the ranch with me. If we're tidying up the woods she's a peewee power house at pushing over dead trees. She's a wonderful person to sit by the fire with, or to ride with or just to be with when the sun goes down or the stars come out. If she ever stopped going to the ranch I'd stop too because I'd see her in every beauty spot there is and I couldn't stand that.

Then there is a sentimental lady I love whose eyes fill up so easily. On the other hand she loves to laugh and her laugh is like tinkling bells. I hear those bells and feel good all over even if I tell a joke she's heard before.

Fortunately all these women in my life are you—fortunately for me that is, for there could be no life for me without you. Browning asked; "How do I love thee—let me count the ways?" For me there is no way to

Dear Mrs. R.   Dec. 25 1981

I still don't feel right about your opening an envelope instead of a gift package.

There are several much beloved women in my life and on Christmas I should be giving them gold, precious stones, perfume, furs and lace. I know that even the best of these would still fall far short of expressing how much these several women mean to me and how empty my life would be without them.

There is of course my "First Lady." She brings so much grace and charm to whatever she does that even stuffy, formal functions sparkle and turn into fun times. Everything is done with class. All I have to do is wash up and show up.

There is another woman in my life who does things I don't always get to see but I hear about them and sometimes see photos of her doing them. She takes an abandoned child in her arms on a hospital visit. The look on her face only the Madonna could match. The look on the childs face is one of adoration. I know because I adore her too.

She bends over a wheelchair or bed to touch an elderly invalid with tenderness and compassion just as she fills my life with warmth and love.

There is another gal I love who is a neat breeder. If she were stuck three days in a hotel room she'd manage to make it home sweet home. She moves things around — looks at it — straightens this and that and you wonder why

Ronnie's Christmas letter, 1981.

THE WHITE HOUSE

WASHINGTON

it wasn't that way in the first place.

I'm also crazy about the girl who goes to the ranch with me. If we're tidying up the woods she's a peewee power house at pushing over dead trees. She's a wonderful person to sit by the fire with, or to ride with or first to be with when the sun goes down or the stars come out. If she ever stopped going to the ranch I'd stop too because I'd see her in every beauty spot there is and I couldn't stand that.

Then there is a sentimental lady I love whose eyes fill up so easily. On the other hand she loves to laugh and her laugh is like tinkling bells. I hear those bells and feel good all over even if I tell a joke she's heard before.

Fortunately all these women in my life are you — fortunately for me that is, for there could be no life for me without you. Browning asked; "How do I love thee - let me count the ways?" For me there is no way to count. I love the whole gang of you — Mommie, first lady, the sentimental you, the fun you and the peewee power house you.

And oh yes, one other very special you — the little girl who takes a "nana" to bed in case she gets hungry in the night. I couldn't & don't sleep well if she isn't there — so please always be there.

Merry Christmas you all — with all my love.

Lucky me.

*count. I love the whole gang of you—Mommie, first lady, the senti-
mental you, the fun you and the peewee power house you.*

*And oh yes, one other very special you—the little girl who takes a
"nana" to bed in case she gets hungry in the night. I couldn't & don't
sleep well if she isn't there—so please always be there.*

Merry Christmas you all—with all my love.

Lucky me.

—

The first week of March 1983 was stressful, to say the very least.
The queen of England had come to California for a rare state visit,
and pretty much everything had gone wrong. The coast was
drenched in torrential rains. The queen was supposed to come visit
us on our ranch in Santa Barbara, but as the days leading up to her
visit passed and the rain continued to fall, this looked more and
more unlikely. The road leading up to the ranch was a very winding
one. There was no visibility at all. When you were in the house, you
couldn't even see out to the fences up front.

We didn't think she would make it, and we were very disap-
pointed, because she and Ronnie had talked about their riding at the
ranch during a weekend we'd spent at Windsor Castle. But the
queen was determined. She got a Land Rover and some boots and
she came right up. We kept apologizing to her—we'd never seen
rain like this before in California!—and she just said, "Don't apolo-
gize. This is an adventure."

We had lunch at the ranch and then navigated our way back down
the hill, and Ronnie had to leave for a meeting in Sacramento. I was

At the ranch in Santa Barbara.

supposed to take the queen for a cruise of the California coastline. The whole thing had been planned so that the *Britannia* would sail into San Francisco harbor as the bridge came up and horns played to welcome her. Of course, none of that took place.

We ended up having to stay in a hotel, which the queen almost never does. Everything had to be rearranged. But sometimes, I think, maybe things that aren't planned come off better than things that are. The visit was very spontaneous and relaxed, in its own way. I remember at one point sitting on a couch after dinner on the *Britannia* with the queen, talking the way any two mothers would talk about their children. That's not something you get to do every day.

ABOARD AIR FORCE ONE   March 4 1983

Dear First Lady

I know tradition has it that on this morning I place cards — Happy Anniversary cards on your breakfast tray. But things are somewhat mixed up. I substituted a gift & delivered it a few weeks ago.

Still this is the day, the day that marks 31 years of such happiness as comes to few men. I told you once it was like an adolescents dream of what marriage should be like. That hasn't changed.

You know I love the ranch — but these last two days made it plain I only love it when you are there. Come to think of it that's true of every place & every time. When you aren't there I'm no place, just lost in time & space.

I more than love you, I'm not whole without you. You are life itself to me. When you are gone I'm waiting for you to return so I can start living again.

Happy Anniversary & thank you for 31 wonderful years. I love you.
                Your grateful husband.

A note from Air Force One.

Things were less pleasant for Ronnie. That week, new labor statistics had come out showing that despite his first administration's best efforts, unemployment was holding steady at over 10 percent. While I accompanied the queen to San Francisco, he had toured flooded areas of the Southern California coast. Then, on March 4, our thirty-first anniversary, he rushed north to join the royal couple and me for dinner aboard the *Britannia* in San Francisco Bay.

He must have been completely exhausted. But by the time he walked off the plane, he had this letter ready and waiting. With so much weighing on his mind, it might seem odd that he'd use his few precious minutes of downtime to write to me. But that's Ronnie!

ABOARD AIR FORCE ONE

March 4 1983

Dear First Lady

I know tradition has it that on this morning I place cards—Happy Anniversary cards on your breakfast tray. But things are somewhat mixed up. I substituted a gift & delivered it a few weeks ago.

Still this is the day, the day that marks 31 years of such happiness as comes to few men. I told you once it was like an adolescent's dream of what marriage should be like. That hasn't changed.

You know I love the ranch—but these last two days made it plain I only love it when you are there. Come to think of it that's true of every place & every time. When you aren't there I'm no place, just lost in time & space.

I more than love you, I'm not whole without you. You are life itself to me. When you are gone I'm waiting for you to return so I can start living again.

Happy Anniversary & thank you for 31 wonderful years.

I love you

Your Grateful Husband

The queen and Prince Philip gave us an engraved silver cigarette box as an anniversary present. I still have it—we had to buy it, of course, when we left the White House. And I still remember Ronnie's toast during dinner: "I know that I promised Nancy everything in the world when we married, but I don't know how I could ever top this!"

———

As far as he was concerned, Ronnie always was my husband first, Mr. President second. He never took himself too seriously. His letters, once signed "Your Ranch Hand," now were signed "Prexy." In his second term, he started signing off as my "roommate," too. This grew out of one of my funnier public mistakes.

We'd had to call off the January 1985 inaugural parade because of bad weather. It was so cold in Washington that year that the doctors said if the marching bands had tried to play their wind instruments, the metal would have stuck to their lips. We felt so bad for all the kids who had saved their money to come to Washington to play that we found a place to have them perform indoors instead.

I was supposed to say a few words to start the festivities off. I said my piece, welcomed the bands, then went back to my seat and sat

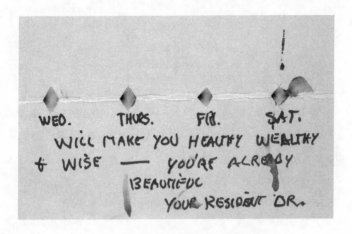

If I was going away on a trip without him,
Ronnie would set out my vitamin pills in advance
and remind me on which days to take them.

down. After a moment, Ronnie leaned over and said, "I think you forgot to introduce me." Oops!

I went back up to the podium and said, "I'd like to intro-duce . . . my husband . . . my roommate, who also happens to be the president of the United States." The crowd loved it. Ronnie loved it too, and afterward, the nickname stuck.

I can never get enough of kissing you. You are the light of my life. I just worship my Roommate—

Your husband

THE WHITE HOUSE
WASHINGTON

Dear Glamour Puss

Welcome home! I missed you. I won't be home til 5:20 and we go to the Nat. Air & Space Museum at 8 P.M. This film will be on the 5 story high screen I've told you about. It will be sensational—you wait and see. We'll be home at 9:10 PM.

I love you mucher and mucher every day.

Your Roommate.

If Ronnie and I hadn't been so close, I don't know how we would have weathered the many sad and frightening experiences we had during the White House years. They run through my mind now—the shooting, the deaths of my father and mother, my breast cancer, Ronnie's colon and prostate cancer, the *Challenger* explosion, the marine-barracks bombing in Lebanon and, of course, Iran-contra. Or the other side of the coin, of course, we had the last Russian summit and the signing of the INF Treaty.

No matter how much power you have as president, there is so much you can't control. Ronnie's last years in office really taught him that. People who were supposedly under his command were off doing things he knew nothing about, and no one ever saw fit to tell him. He was badly served by the people who were supposed to aid and advise him.

THE WHITE HOUSE
WASHINGTON

Dear Glamour Puss

Welcome home! I missed you.
I won't be home til 5:20 and
we go to the Nat. Air & Space
Museum at 8 P.M. This film
will be on the 5 story high
screen I've told you about. It
will be sensational — you wait &
see. We'll be home at 9:10 P.M.

I love you mucher & mucher
every day.

Your Room mate.

In 1987, when the pope came to California.

Despite all the challenges, we were sad to leave the White House when Ronnie's second term came to an end in 1989. We'd both been happy there. We'd become very attached to the White House, the ushers, and the staff—everyone. They didn't care about what party you were with; they just loved the White House, and they'd been thrilled by all the work we'd done to fix things up and give the place back its former grandeur. I'll never forget how, right after the renovations were done, one of the butlers who had been there a long, long time looked down the hall and said, "*This* is how the White House should look." That was one of my proudest moments as first lady. It was my Oscar.

I also had such wonderful memories of our state dinners, which we tried to hold every month or two. Whenever possible, I'd have them outside, directly under the night sky. That was really magical. I'd put little white lights in the trees around the Rose Garden, and if we were lucky, there was moonlight, and starlight, then the lights of the White House and of the Jefferson Memorial. It was beautiful, just beautiful. And on great occasions, like the state dinner for the Gorbachevs that followed the Washington summit meeting of December 1987, it was very, very moving, too.

—

Our last few weeks in Washington were filled with good-byes, many of them very difficult. We hated to leave our new friends. They'd done so much to welcome us eight years earlier—and they gave us such a gracious send-off, too. I'll never forget, for example, the last time we went to the Kennedy Center. After the show, Walter Cronkite came out onstage and said, "For eight years, two people have sat up there in that box alongside our honorees. The years have gone swiftly by, but, President and Mrs. Reagan, we'd like to detain you long enough to say thank you."

Then everybody came out onstage—all the stagehands and all the people connected to the Kennedy Center. All the ushers came down the aisles, and they and everyone in the audience turned

Valentine's Day card.

around, faced us, and started to sing "Auld Lang Syne." That's a song that does me in under any circumstance. And, of course, I started to cry.

Ronnie waited until everyone had finished singing. Then he shouted down to Cronkite, "It beats getting an Oscar!"

In the hammock at the ranch, 1980s.

On our last morning in the White House, Ronnie had gone over to the Oval Office to have a last look. I have a picture that we took then—all of his papers were gone and the office looked so bare. Then, all too quickly, it was ten o'clock and the Bushes were there. It was time for us to leave. As we were leaving the White House for the last time and walking to the plane, Ronnie turned to me with his wonderful grin and said, "Well, it's been a wonderful eight years. All in all, not bad—not bad at all."

As our helicopter took off, the pilots circled over the White House so we could see it once more. "Look, honey," Ronnie said. "There's our little bungalow."

—

Air Force One took us back to California. When we landed in Los Angeles, there was a band at the airport and our old friends were there to meet us. Fortunately, our new home in Bel Air was all ready.

Ronnie had only visited the new house once before. I'd been in charge of house hunting and had been told about this one by a friend and had made a trip to California to visit it. I'd liked it, but obviously, I wasn't going to buy a house without Ronnie's seeing it. Getting a president to make a discreet house visit, though, isn't an easy thing. I had to find a way for him to see it without the press catching on and making a big fuss. I didn't think that was the best way to make friends with the neighbors, either.

So one time when we'd gone to California, I'd decided to smuggle him in. We left our hotel and I persuaded him to get down on the floor of the car, out of sight. "You have to stay there," I said. We got up to the house, and I took him through it so fast that I'm sure he didn't really get a good look. He said, "I like it," and then we got back into the car and we left, with the president of the United States on the car floor!

Now, when we walked in, there were boxes everywhere. I had a sinking feeling. It wasn't a very big house ("I've *already* lived in a big house," I'd told the realtors), but there still was so much to do. I got very sad when Tim McCarthy, the Secret Service man who'd been shot with Ronnie, had to leave. I started to cry, and said, "I don't want you to go."

I've often heard people say that it's a trauma to leave the White House and adjust to life after the presidency. For Ronnie and me it was an adjustment, certainly. But a trauma? No. Ronnie never had a problem changing from one phase of life to the other. I think that's because no matter what he's doing or where he is in the world, he is always the same. And as far as I was concerned, everything was always fine as long as he was there.

We ended up loving our new home. Ronnie said that of all the

My Darling

Having everything I could ever want for Christmas and every day as long as I have you I'd like to package the world but it wont go through the chimney. In the meantime you'll have to settle for this & the fact that I love you more & more each day.

Poppa

A Christmas card.

For My Sweetheart
ON VALENTINE'S DAY

You know that I love you
And you must know, too,
That my happiest moments
Are those spent with you.
For when we're together
Or when we're apart,
You're first in my thoughts
And you're first in my heart.

Happy Valentine's Day
With Love

Every Word of it - every
word of it !! — Guess Who —
I'm first to your left if you
need a hint.

houses we'd lived in, it was his favorite, which of course made me happy. We planned to split our time between Bel Air and our ranch, writing our memoirs, speaking out for the causes we believed in, riding horses, seeing friends and traveling. And at first that was the life that we had. We traveled some, toured the inland waterways of Alaska with friends, and just generally resumed our life together. We had fun. We had so many things to look back on together and enjoy.

On one anniversary, looking ahead to a happy day together in 2002, Ronnie wrote:

> *To the One Woman in my Life*
> *Fifty years isn't enough. Let's carry on*
> *Your happy happy husband.*

Our life was to change soon, though, and to change irrevocably—and neither of us saw it coming.

Christmas 1998, with Maureen and Dennis.

In July 1989, Ronnie and I went down to Mexico to visit our friends Betty and Bill Wilson at their ranch. I remember that on one of our first days there, Ronnie looked up in the sky and saw a helicopter overhead. "What's that?" he said.

"It's the Secret Service," I answered. "They're trying to figure out where they could land a plane if they had to."

Thank goodness they did.

A few days later, Ronnie went out riding. I was working on my memoir, *My Turn,* and decided to stay behind. I was sitting in the house when all of a sudden the Secret Service men came running toward me. As if by instinct, I found myself running, too.

Ronnie had been thrown off his horse. He was riding with some other men, going up an incline, when one of the ranch hands had hit something that made a loud noise and spooked Ronnie's horse.

The horse reared once, and Ronnie stayed on. It reared a second time, and Ronnie stayed on again. Two Secret Service men tried to move in and calm the horse, but they couldn't do it. The horse reared a third time, bucking so hard that Ronnie fell off and hit his head on the ground, miraculously missing the jagged rocks all around.

We got him on a plane and immediately took him to a hospital in Tucson, Arizona. He should really have stayed there, but it was my birthday and the Wilsons had planned a celebration, and Ronnie was determined to go back to the ranch. We went back—but at my insistence, we took a doctor with us.

The day after my birthday, we flew home. I was very uneasy and kept at Ronnie until he agreed to get his head X-rayed. We went to the Mayo Clinic, where we'd gone every year for our checkups. It turned out that Ronnie had a concussion and a subdural hematoma. He needed to be operated on right away. It all happened so quickly that I think, once again, I was in shock. It shows up in the picture that appeared in the press at the time: Ronnie leaving the hospital, taking his hat off to salute the crowd, and me dashing forward trying to cover his partially shaven head with my hand. He didn't care that he had no hair on one side—but I did!

I've always had the feeling that the severe blow to his head in 1989 hastened the onset of Ronnie's Alzheimer's. The doctors think so, too. In the years leading up to the diagnosis of the disease, in August 1994, he had not shown symptoms of the illness. I didn't suspect that Ronnie was ill when we went back to the Mayo Clinic that summer for our regular checkup. When the doctors told us they'd found symptoms of Alzheimer's, I was dumbfounded. Ronnie's fall from the horse had worried me terribly, of course, and I'd had to urge him to take time out to recover after his operation. But I had seen no signs of anything else.

I also didn't realize at the time what an Alzheimer's diagnosis really meant. It's a disease that people are still not terribly knowl-

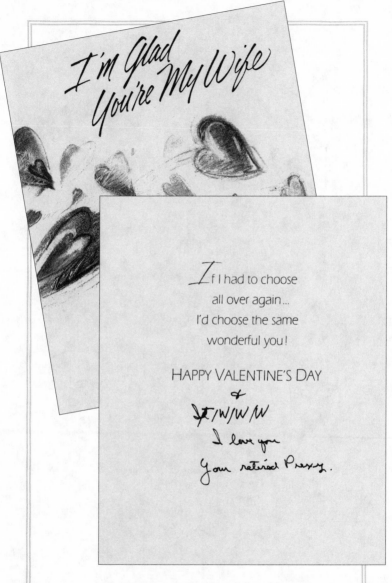

I'm Glad You're My Wife

*I*f I had to choose
all over again...
I'd choose the same
wonderful you!

HAPPY VALENTINE'S DAY

&

It/W/W/W
I love you
Your retired Prexy.

A Valentine from "your retired Prexy," 1990.

THERE I WAS DOODLING AWAY — THEN
I BEGAN TO THINK ABOUT YOU.
SO-O-O-O..

NDB
RR

*Another doodle that I love. I had this one framed,
too, and keep it on my desk.*

edgeable about, and a few years ago, they were even less so. Families treated it like a dark secret, so people—the patients and their families—suffered in isolation. It's only recently that people have started to speak out and to treat it as a disease like any other.

The diagnosis didn't sink in for a while. Neither one of us really knew what was going to happen, but of course we knew it wasn't good. Ronnie reacted the way he always has with everything—he just went ahead and dealt with it. Like most people then, I didn't know much about Alzheimer's (looking back, I suppose this was just as well), but I was certainly going to learn! I got the book *The 36-Hour Day*, which is given to caregivers, and sent one to each of the children so that they could learn more about the disease, too.

I have often in recent years recalled a conversation Ronnie had with Cardinal Cooke shortly after the shooting in 1981. "God was certainly sitting on your shoulder that day," the cardinal said. Ronnie replied, "Yes, I know, and whatever days are left to me, they belong to Him."

Once in a while I would wonder whether that conversation played a part in Ronnie's decision to write his beautiful letter to the American people about his Alzheimer's. After the shooting, both of us always went public with our health problems when we were in the White House. We believed strongly that it helped people—and it did. When Ronnie talked about his colon cancer, more people went to be tested. When I talked about my breast cancer, more women had mammograms. So when we heard this diagnosis, Ronnie once again thought about ways that his own experience could help other people. And I do think that writing the letter served the purpose he hoped for: More people now understand that Alzheimer's is a disease like any other and not a reason to be embarrassed or self-conscious, and research has increased.

Ronnie wrote the Alzheimer's letter at a table in the library and gave it to me to read before it was released. I was surprised when people later asked who had drafted the letter, because it seemed so clear to me that they were his words, that it was his natural way of writing.

It is difficult to describe my life now. People are incredibly kind and sympathetic—in an elevator, on the street, everywhere. And the mail, which is tremendous, reflects the same concerns and feelings. I can't begin to say how much this means to me and how helpful it is. First of all, there is a feeling of loneliness when you're in this situation. Not that your friends aren't supportive of you; they are. But no one can really know what it's like unless they've traveled this path—and there are many right now traveling the same path I am. You know that it's a progressive disease and that there's no place to go but down, no light at the end of the tunnel. You get tired and frustrated, because you have no control and you feel helpless. We've had an extraordinary life, and I've been blessed to have been married for almost fifty years to a man I deeply love—but the other side of the coin is that it makes it harder. There are so many memories that I can no longer share, which makes it very difficult. When it comes right down to it, you're in it alone. Each day is different, and you get up, put one foot in front of the other, and go—and love; just love.

I try to remember Ronnie telling me so many times that God has a plan for us which we don't understand now but one day will, or my mother saying that you play the hand that's dealt you. It's hard, but

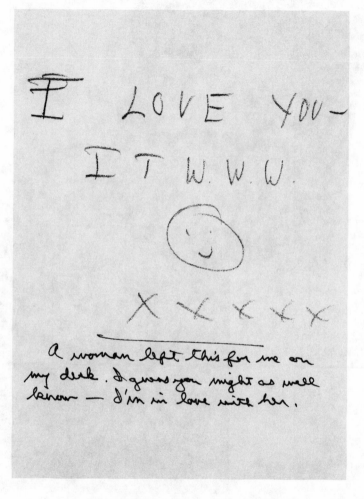

A note I left for Ronnie—and his reply.

THIS PAGE AND TOP RIGHT:
Ronnie working outdoors at Rancho del Cielo.

Riding at Rancho del Cielo.

even now there are moments Ronnie has given me that I wouldn't trade for anything. Alzheimer's is a truly long, long good-bye. But it's the living out of love.

November 5, 1994

My Fellow Americans,

I have recently been told that I am one of the millions of Americans who will be afflicted with Alzheimer's Disease.

Upon learning this news, Nancy & I had to decide whether as private citizens we would keep this a private matter or whether we would make this news known in a public way.

In the past Nancy suffered from breast cancer and I had my cancer surgeries. We found through our open disclosures we were able to raise public awareness. We were happy that as a result many more people underwent testing.

They were treated in early stages and able to return to normal, healthy lives.

So now, we feel it is important to share it with you. In opening our hearts, we hope this might promote greater awareness of this condition. Perhaps it will encourage a clearer understanding of the individuals and families who are affected by it.

At the moment I feel just fine. I intend to live the remainder of the years God gives me on this earth doing the things I have always done. I will continue to share life's journey with my beloved Nancy and my family. I plan to enjoy the great outdoors and stay in touch with my friends and supporters.

Unfortunately, as Alzheimer's Disease progresses, the family often bears a heavy burden. I only wish there was some way I could spare Nancy from this painful experience. When the time comes I am confident that with your help she will face it with faith and courage.

In closing let me thank you, the American people, for giving me the great honor of allowing me to serve as your President. When the Lord calls me home, whenever that may be, I will leave with the greatest love for this country of ours and eternal optimism for its future.

I now begin the journey that will lead me into the sunset of my life. I know that for America there will always be a bright dawn ahead.

Thank you my friends. May God always bless you.

Sincerely,

Ronald Reagan

Kissing Ronnie "Happy Birthday,"
February 6, 2000.